The Authors

Maralene and Miles Wesner are multi-talented teachers and prolific writers. They have published more than 150 Audio-Visual Education aids, and pioneered new reading methods with their Phonics in a Nutshell (1965).

They have written articles, and mission studies for Southern Baptist periodicals. They were in the original group of writers to develop WMU's Big "A" Club material.

They've published several books with Broadman Press: *A Fresh Look at the Gospel* (1983); *You Are What You Choose* (1984); and *How To Be a Saint When You Feel Like a Sinner* (1986) and self-published 30 books by Diversity Press.

They are noted for their no-nonsense style, their clear illustrations, and their willingness to face controversial issues. From the dual perspectives of both academic and religious professions, they seek to be a bridge between the spiritual and the intellectual worlds.

They hold Masters Degrees (MEd) from Oklahoma University plus work toward a Doctorate. Miles also attended Southwestern Baptist Theological Seminary, and served as a high school counselor. He has been the bi-vocational pastor of a small rural church for more than 50 years.

Both Maralene and Miles taught in public school and collages and served as educational consultants. Maralene taught Psychology and Speech for Southeastern Oklahoma State University for 32 years. She was chosen Oklahoma Teacher of the Year in 1975.

They have planned, led tours, and done research in all of the 50 states, Canada, Mexico, Europe, Egypt, Japan, and the Holy Land. In 1985, they were among a small group of Americans who were invited by Dr. Joseph P. Kennedy of the US/China Education Foundation and Bishop Ting, leader of the Three Self Movement, to participate in the First Symposium on the Church in Nanjing, China.

Now, they use their lifetime of varied experiences to write insightful sermons, essays, and books.

Titles by Maralene & Miles Wesner
published by Nurturing Faith

Sermons for Special Days

Life More Abundant

Do You Really Know Jesus?

If Jesus Were Here Today

101 Sparks of Inspiration

101 *Sparks* OF INSPIRATION

Scripture-Based Sermon Starters
and Devotions

Maralene & Miles Wesner

© 2022
Published in the United States by Nurturing Faith, Macon, GA.
Nurturing Faith is a book imprint of Good Faith Media (goodfaithmedia.org).
Library of Congress Cataloging-in-Publication Data is available.

ISBN: 978-1-63528-193-4

All rights reserved. Printed in the United States of America.

Scripture quotations are from New Revised Standard Version Bible, copyright © 1989 National Council of the Churches of Christ in the United States of America. Used by permission. All rights reserved worldwide.

Scriptures marked KJV are taken from the KING JAMES VERSION (KJV): KING JAMES VERSION, public domain.

Cover photograph by David Cassady.

Contents

Preface..............................1

1: Abundant Life Is Available
2: Almost Persuaded
3: Analyzing Your DNA
4: Are You Alive?
5: Are You Mad, Sad, or Glad?
6: Arranging Priorities
7: Behind Closed Doors
8: Belief Is Not Enough
9: Bitter or Better?
10: Change Is Possible
11: Children Are Different
12: Christian Liberty
13: A Church Full of Pauls
14: Church Growth
15: Common Copouts
16: Conceiving, Believing, Achieving
17: Could I? Should I? Would I?
18: Cutting Out the Middleman
19: Don't Blame Me
20: Down but Not Out!
21: The Edge of the Unknown
22: Emotional Paupers
23: Excuses, Excuses, Excuses!
24: Failure Is Not Final!
25: Faith Needs Feet
26: Five Rules for Living
27: Five Steps to Faith
28: Fixers and Fanatics?
29: Forgiveness
30: Forgive Their Ignorance
31: Four Basic Needs
32: Giving for the Right Reason
33: God Knows Your Name
34: God's Plan for You
35: The Gospel in a Nutshell
36: Handling Anger
37: Handling Difficult People
38: Happiness
39: Hiding or Healing?
40: The Holy Spirit
41: How to Be a Light
42: How to Fight Fair
43: How to Slay Giants
44: How to Spell Faith
45: Is Bigger Always Better?
46: Jesus's Ministry Methods

47: Jesus Respects Diversity
48: The Language of the People
49: Leaders or Charlatans?
50: Learning from the Animals
51: Lessons of Life
52: Letters from God
53: Leveling and Listening
54: Little Things Mean a Lot
55: Logic
56: Looking for What's Wrong
57: Love Your Enemies!
58: The Lure of Certainty
59: Masks, Armors, and Spears
60: Ministering Angels
61: Moral "I" Tests
62: Nobody's Perfect!
63: No Place to Hide
64: Of Complaints and Compliments
65: Of Sowing and Reaping
66: Our Great Potential
67: Pastor/Laymen Partnerships
68: People Need People
69: The Prodigal Son's Father
70: The Pursuit of Happiness
71: Rageholics
72: Retaliation or Annihilation
73: Seven Fundamentals of Faith
74: Sharing the Key
75: Sins of Omission
76: The Status of Christians
77: Steps to Failure
78: The Strange Gospel of Jesus
79: Sunny Days or Stormy Nights?
80: Talk or Walk?
81: Three Principles of Behavior
82: Three Useless Expressions
83: Trash, Trinkets, or Treasures?
84: Unanswered Prayers
85: The Upside-Down Gospel
86: Using Our Strengths
87: Using Plan B!
88: Wash-Basin Religion
89: We Are Witnesses
90: What Do We Really Want?
91: What Is Love?
92: What Is the Gospel?
93: What Moves Us?
94: What Should I Feel?
95: What the World Needs Now!
96: What to Do with Hostility
97: Whited Sepulchers
98: Why Am I Mad?
99: Why Do Adults Say No?
100: You Are Valuable!
101: Z Is for Zeal

Preface

Many churches today have lay ministers or bivocational pastors. These dedicated leaders often work at secular jobs yet must prepare two or three sermons a week. This can be a real challenge.

Most of the brief compositions in this book can stand alone as quick devotionals, or they can be used as "sermon starters" by providing suggested topics and outlines that include extensive scriptural research. This saves leaders and teachers time, but still allows them to add their own special insights, develop their own applications, and adapt the material to their own personal style.

All of these "starters" were originally used in a small rural church where we served as bivocational pastors for more than fifty years.

1: Abundant Life Is Available

Jesus said, "I came that they may have life and have it abundantly" (John 10:10). What, then, are the characteristics of those with abundant life?

1. *They have priorities.* They can separate the significant from the trivial, and emphasize issues that are within their areas of expertise and responsibility. Jesus said, "But strive first for the kingdom of God and his righteousness, and all these things will be given to you as well" (Matt 6:33).

2. *They have focus.* They set specific goals and zero in on a few major projects instead of fragmenting their energy on irrelevant sidetracks and detours. Paul said, "I do not consider that I have made it my own; but this one thing I do: forgetting what lies behind and straining forward to what lies ahead, I press on toward the goal" (Phil 3:13–14).

3. *They have timing.* They avoid impulsive acts and practice deferred gratification patterns. They've learned to enjoy anticipation and are willing to endure delays. They know that going into debt is like grabbing one dollar today when they could have had ten dollars by waiting until tomorrow. Scripture says, "Let us also lay aside every weight and the sin that clings so closely, and let us run with perseverance the race that is set before us" (Heb 12:1).

4. *They have limits.* They stay within moral and financial guidelines. They don't overextend their roles. They know they can only control things within their own arena. Solomon said, "Keep sound wisdom and prudence" (Prov 3:21). He also said, "Like a city breached, without walls, is one who lacks self-control" (Prov 25:28).

5. *They have persistence.* They don't start more than they can finish. They complete worthwhile projects as soon as possible. They would rather feel the accomplishment of doing one thing well than the excitement of having a dozen unrealistic pipedreams. Paul said, "Let us not grow weary in doing what is right, for we will reap at harvest time, if we do not give up" (Gal 6:9).

In order to develop these traits that promise abundant life, a person must have a relationship with Jesus.

2: Almost Persuaded

Almost is a sad and incomplete word. It means "nearly" or "not quite," "less than successful." *Almost* is a term describing a feeling of frustration and regret. It refers to an opportunity missed. It defines an attempted achievement that was, unfortunately, a total failure.

There are many "almost" people in the Bible:

Pharaoh, who contradicted his stand repeatedly before Moses led the children of Israel out of Egypt;

Herod, who heard John gladly yet ordered him beheaded;

Judas, who ate with Jesus and afterward betrayed him;

Pilate, who would have let Jesus go but for his friendship with Caesar;

Felix, who quaked as he shrank from the influence of the Holy Spirit;

Agrippa, who uttered those fateful words, "Almost thou persuadest me to be a Christian" (Acts 26:28 KJV).

People say, "I *almost* went to college"; "I *almost* got a job"; "I *almost* married my sweetheart." Strangely enough, they still don't have a degree, or a salary, or a mate.

Almost is an empty word without profit or advantage. Of what value is it if it *almost* rains or if the sun *almost* shines? Can a man overcome hunger by *almost* eating, alleviate thirst by *almost* drinking, or become a Christian by *almost* making a commitment?

Paul didn't say, "I have *almost* finished my race" or "I have *almost* kept the faith." Instead, he said, "I have fought the good fight, I have finished the race, I have kept the faith" (2 Tim 4:7).

Jesus didn't say, "I have *almost* finished the work you gave me to do." Instead, he said, "I glorified you on earth by finishing the work that you gave me to do" (John 17:4).

Almost doesn't bring crowns or glory. Don't be an almost person!

3: Analyzing Your DNA

Your DNA is absolutely unique. We know that's true in the physical realm, but it's also true in the emotional realm.

1. D *represents your desires*. What do you really want? From your simplest food and recreation choices to your deepest emotional longings, you are unique. The psalmist said, "Take delight in the LORD, and he will give you the desires of your heart" (Ps 37:4).

2. N *represents your needs*. What frustrates you, and what fulfills you? From your normal requirements for food and sleep to your most passionate obsessions, you are unique. Jesus said, "Do not worry, saying, 'What will we eat?' or 'What will we drink?' or 'What will we wear?'… Seek first the kingdom of God and his righteousness, and all these things will be given to you as well" (Matt 6:31, 33).

3. A *represents your abilities*. What can you do that no one else can do? From your ordinary skills with tools to your greatest creative talents, you are unique. Paul said, "We have gifts that differ according to the grace given to us" (Rom 12:6).

"There are varieties of gifts but the same Spirit" (1 Cor 12:4).

"Do not neglect the gift that is in you" (1 Tim 4:14).

Analyze your "DNA." Find your interests and passions and deepest desires. Discover your insecurities and cravings and basic needs. Develop your strengths and proficiencies and special abilities.

You are valuable and unique!

4: Are You Alive?

Are you alive? might seem like an odd question, but when Jesus dealt with the issue of life and death, he meant something more than mere physical existence. John said, "Whoever has the Son has life; whoever does not have the Son of God does not have life" (1 John 5:12).

It's obvious that this kind of life isn't something we can only hope for in heaven. It is a real and present possession; we can have it now! Paul said, "When you were dead in trespasses…God made you alive together with him" (Col 2:13).

So what are the characteristics of life?

1. L *is for* love. John said, "We know that we have passed from death to life because we love the brothers and sisters" (1 John 3:14a).

Love includes understanding and compassion. Do you truly and deeply love others?

2. I *is for* insight. Jesus said, "To you it has been given to know the secrets of the kingdom of heaven" (Matt 13:11).

Insight includes awareness and wisdom. Do you have intuitive understanding?

3. F *is for* feelings. Paul said, "They should seek the Lord, if haply they might feel after him, and find him" (Acts 17:27 KJV).

Feelings include sensitivity and empathy. Do you experience emotional honesty?

4. E *is for* enjoyment. Jesus said, "I have said these things to you so that my joy may be in you and that your joy may be complete" (John 15:11). Enjoyment includes contentment and happiness. Do you delight in the essence of each moment?

Are you really alive?

Jesus can give you life. He said, "I came that they may have life and have it abundantly" (John 10:10).

5: Are You Mad, Sad, or Glad?

When we think we're angry, we're usually feeling something else.

1. *We feel anger when we're hurt.* We may be hurt because someone didn't fulfill our needs. Anger is merely used as a coverup. It's considered more macho to pound the table than to admit honest feelings. If an acquaintance doesn't speak, I feel angry. But I'm really hurt because I needed their recognition. If a friend criticizes me, I'm hurt because I needed their approval. If a spouse forgets an anniversary, I'm hurt because I needed their love.

The prodigal son's older brother is an example of unjustified anger. His hateful attitude was caused by envy and jealousy, which were based on hurt feelings. He said, "For all these years I have been working like a slave for you, and I have never disobeyed your command, yet you have never given me even a young goat so that I might celebrate with my friends. But when this son of yours came back, who has devoured your assets with prostitutes, you killed the fatted calf for him!" (Luke 15:29–30).

The older brother was hurt because he thought his father loved his brother more. We feel anger when we're hurt.

2. *We feel anger when we're embarrassed.* We may be embarrassed because some weakness or failure was revealed. If my son wears odd clothing, I feel angry. But I'm really embarrassed because my friends will think we're weird. If my toddler has a temper tantrum in the supermarket, I'm angry. But I'm really embarrassed because other people will think I'm a bad parent. If a bill collector comes to repossess my television, I'm embarrassed because the neighbors will think I'm a poor provider.

Jonah was angry at the whole world when his congregation repented and avoided destruction! He was angry when a worm ate a vine that was shading him (see Jon 4:6–8). When God questioned his anger, he responded with more anger, saying, "Yes, angry enough to die" (Jon 4:9).

His selfish and hostile mood was caused by embarrassment because his prophecy of doom did not occur. We feel anger when we're embarrassed.

3. *We feel anger when we're afraid.* We may be afraid because there is danger of a potential loss. If my teenager is two hours late coming home, I

feel angry. But I'm really afraid. I imagine wrecks and hospitals and morgues. If a driver runs me off the road and I almost collide with another car, I feel angry. But I'm really afraid. I was almost killed! If my spouse gets a call from an unknown member of the opposite sex, I feel angry. But I'm really afraid that there's an affair going on! What if my home and marriage and livelihood are at risk?

The Jews were angry at Jesus because he was a threat to their traditions. They feared change. Jesus said, "Are you angry with me because I healed a man's whole body on the Sabbath?" (John 7:23).

We feel angry when we're hurt, embarrassed, or afraid. *Our insecurities make us angry.*

So when we're angry, we should ask ourselves, "Am I hurt? Why? What expectation did I have that wasn't met? Was it a valid expectation? What can I do about it? Can I get it met, or can I learn to live without it being met?"

We should ask ourselves, "Am I embarrassed? Why? What weakness was I trying to hide? Should it be hidden? Is it something that would really bring on undeserved disgrace? Or is it something that would bring on legitimate guilt? What can I do about it? Can I leave it in my past and go on? Or can I admit it and rectify it?"

We should ask ourselves, "Am I afraid? Why? What loss do I fear? What status or possession of mine is being threatened? Is this a real or an imaginary threat? What can I do about it? Can I protect myself from the possible loss? Or can I rearrange my attitudes and accommodate myself to life without this thing?"

Let's always analyze our angry reactions to find the cause. This will help us handle this powerful emotion in a productive way.

6: Arranging Priorities

Years ago, a mental institution used a simple test for releasing inmates. The director turned on a water faucet and let the sink overflow. Then he sent the patient in to solve the problem. If he began to mop without turning off the water, he wasn't ready for dismissal. If he immediately turned off the water and then mopped, he was considered to be sane.

You see, putting first things first and arranging priorities is an important thinking skill. Jesus often asked, "What do you think?" (e.g., Luke 10:36).

What we think about is important, but *how* we think is even more so.

1. *Think broadly.* Ask yourself: Is this a specific physical need, or is this a universal spiritual need?

Jesus said, "Do not keep seeking what you are to eat and what you are to drink, and do not keep worrying.... Instead, seek his kingdom, and these things will be given to you as well" (Luke 12:29, 31).

Ask yourself: Do my priorities deal with trivial things or broad issues that affect many people?

2. *Think deeply.* Ask yourself: Is this a superficial need, or is it a basic profound need?

Paul said, "While physical training is of some value, godliness is valuable in every way, holding promise for both the present life and the life to come" (1 Tim 4:8).

Ask yourself: Do my priorities deal with shallow things or with deep issues that have great significance for humanity?

3. *Think long term.* Ask yourself: Is this an immediate need, or is it a long-term, permanent need?

Paul said, "We look not at what can be seen but at what cannot be unseen, for what can be seen is temporary, but what cannot be seen is eternal" (2 Cor 4:18).

Ask yourself: Do my priorities deal with immediate things or with issues that have long-term benefit for others? Arrange your priorities before it's too late.

7: Behind Closed Doors

Everybody has a history, a hurt, and a hope. That's the story of mankind. That's the biography of humanity. That's the drama of life.

Almost every family has a secret, an unopened closet, a Pandora's box, a hidden skeleton. Almost every family has its black sheep, its hush-hush conversations, and its subjects that are just not talked about.

There are physical, mental, emotional, and sexual abuse issues. There is alcoholism, drug addiction, and mental illness. There is illegitimacy, abortion, and divorce. There are crimes, affairs, and bankruptcies. No one escapes. Almost everybody has a link with some sin that society condemns. Therefore, almost everybody feels they are living a lie. Furthermore, almost everybody feels they're the only one in the world who has this particular problem.

Such deception destroys our self-worth, sabotages our social relationships, and nullifies our productivity. It forces us to pretend, cover up, and wear a mask.

Why do we feel we must put on a front? Why are we so afraid of revealing our flaws? Why do we think we're the only ones with weaknesses? This charade of perfect people, perfect families, and perfect lives is so unnecessary.

As creatures of this earth, we all share fallibilities. None of us is omniscient or omnipotent. In fact, we're much more alike under the skin than we might think. Maybe we could relax and be real if people weren't so prone to judgment. We're not here to criticize, humiliate, evaluate, and fix each other. We're not here to point out shortcomings, flaws, and faults in our associates.

On the contrary, we're here to help, lift, and encourage. We're here to form connections. We're here to rejoice together and weep together.

Yes, everybody has a history, a hurt, and a hope. Let's not hide these things behind closed doors.

1. *Let's recall our history.* "Remember, then, from what you have fallen; repent and do the works you did at first" (Rev 2:5).

2. *Let's admit our hurts.* "If we confess our sins, he who is faithful and just will forgive us our sins and cleanse us from all unrighteousness" (1 John 1:9)

3. *Let's express our hopes.* "May the God of hope fill you with all joy and peace in believing, so that you may abound in hope by the power of the Holy Spirit" (Rom 15:13).

It's only when we recall our history, admit our hurts, and express our hopes that we can truly live and learn and grow.

Now, this doesn't mean we're to tell everything we know. It doesn't mean we're to parade our "dirty linen" in public. It certainly doesn't mean we're to bring shame on others by betraying confidences. It does mean, however, that we can accept ourselves, even with our imperfections, as worthwhile persons. It does mean we can feel free to either share our hurts or analyze them and let them go.

There's great comfort and liberation in discovering that every household has its closet with the closed door. Almost every individual has a link with some hidden sin. So even when our history is sordid, our hurts excruciating, and our hope almost nonexistent, we can be sure that we are not alone.

8: Belief Is Not Enough

"Faith," said the little girl, "is believing what you know ain't so."

We emphasize belief, but do we understand it? On several occasions Jesus himself said belief isn't enough! The scriptures say, "Many believed in his name because they saw the signs.... But Jesus...would not entrust himself to them, because he knew all people" (see John 2:23–24).

What was wrong with these people's belief? They seemed to be sincere. They had the correct formula. They were focused on the proper object. Yet the Lord didn't commit himself to them. No conversion occurred. No relationship developed. No spiritual life resulted.

This is very confusing. Are there different kinds of belief? Well, James says there are. He said, "You believe that God is one; you do well. Even the demons believe—and shudder.... Faith apart from works is worthless" (Jas 2:19–20).

Rational belief alone isn't enough. Emotional belief alone isn't enough. What we need is a faith for every day: one that can be transferred from worship to work, one that's relevant instead of theoretical, one that's based on common sense instead of complicated theology.

A professor once said, "If you lack grace, God can provide it. If you lack knowledge, I can provide it. But if you lack common sense, neither the good Lord nor I can help you!"

So when is belief not enough?

When It Lacks Sincerity

Jesus said, "You are those who justify yourselves in the sight of others, but God knows your hearts, for what is prized by humans is an abomination in the sight of God" (Luke 16:15).

Too often, our beliefs are merely teachings we've heard all our lives and never questioned. This won't do. Faith must be personal.

What's the bottom line in your life? What do you live for? What would you die for? That's your faith! Belief is not enough unless it's sincere and genuine.

When It Lacks Consistency

James said, "Ask in faith, never doubting, for the one who doubts is like a wave of the sea, driven and tossed by the wind. For the doubter, being double-minded and unstable in every way, must not expect to receive anything from the Lord" (Jas 1:6–7).

Off and on devotion and hot and cold emotions are worthless. They can't change your attitude or motivate your behavior.

Suppose you got into a taxi in New York City and told the driver to take you to the Empire State Building. After a block or two, you told him to drive you to Central Park. After a couple more blocks, you asked him to go to Wall Street. You could hardly expect to get anywhere. The cab driver would soon dump you out on the street.

Some Christians are like that. They express faith and practice doubt. Belief is not enough unless it is consistent and permanent!

When It Lacks Commitment

James said, "Someone will say, 'You have faith, and I have works.' Show me your faith apart from your works, and I by my works will show you faith" (Jas 2:18).

Paul said, "They profess to know God, but they deny him by their actions" (Titus 1:16).

We don't really believe unless we live according to our beliefs. Christianity is not an idea to be believed. It's a life to be lived.

9: Bitter or Better?

All of us get hurt sooner or later. It's a fact of life. So the question is not, "Will you get hurt?" The question is, "How will you handle it when you do get hurt?"

Suppose someone tells lies about you and ruins your reputation? Suppose someone rejects you or neglects you? Suppose someone keeps you from getting a job or a promotion?

Hurt comes in all shapes and sizes. Sometimes we're tempted to withdraw into our shell so we can never be hurt again. Unfortunately, this creates cynicism. If you become numb to hurt, you also become numb to love and joy.

In fact, the hurt usually starts out as a slight, an unkind word, a false accusation, or a broken promise. When this happens, we have a choice. We can dismiss it and go on, or we can let the disease of "grudgery" take over. An emotional wound can heal, or it can become infected. A serious wound that's allowed to heal is not nearly so destructive as a minor wound that gets infected. Paul said, "Put away from you all bitterness and wrath and anger and wrangling and slander, together with all malice" (Eph 4:31).

Most of us nourish bitterness because we think it gives us some kind of revenge. We imagine that "awful person" will feel the force of our wrath and suffer from it. But they don't! Most of those people we are trying to punish couldn't care less. Our attitude doesn't bother them at all.

In fact, the moment we start hating a person, we become his slave. We can't succeed at work because he controls our thoughts. We don't enjoy life because stress makes us miserable.

The person we hate follows us wherever we go. He spoils our appetite and ruins our sleep.

Momentary anger is inevitable, but letting that anger smolder into bitterness is different. No matter what has happened, we can choose to forgive. Bitterness, like a poisonous plant, requires soil and nutrients to grow. Remove the soil of resentment and the nutrients of self-pity and it will die.

A hurting person may protest, "But you don't know how I feel!" That's true, but Jesus does, and he's the one who said, "Father, forgive [those who are crucifying me], for they do not know what they are doing" (Luke 23:34).

So when we're hurt, we can either let bitterness destroy our lives, or we can forgive and go on. Forgiveness is not only the right thing to do; it's the smart thing to do. This doesn't mean pretending you haven't been hurt. Rather, it means choosing to grow beyond the pain. Your hurts can make you bitter or better. It's your choice!

10: Change Is Possible

Jeremiah said, "Can Cushites change their skin or leopards their spots? Then also you can do good who are accustomed to do evil" (Jer 13:23).

Change is possible, but it's certainly not easy. In fact, change puts more stress on an organism than anything else. Change is difficult because we become conditioned to certain situations and familiar with certain ideas. We grow accustomed to certain habits. Unless something happens to force a change, we continue to operate as usual.

Few people change voluntarily. Jesus said, "The gate is narrow and the road is hard that leads to life, and there are few who find it" (Matt 7:14). If you are one of those courageous individuals who is willing to change, there are three steps to be taken:

Mental Change

We must use our intellect to determine how the undesirable attitude or behavior began. We must analyze its causes and understand why it continues. We must discover what current persons, places, or events trigger it.

Emotional Change

Knowing intellectually that a reaction is irrational or unproductive doesn't necessarily eliminate it. We must identify our feelings and describe them as precisely as we can. Then we must express our concerns clearly and honestly to a caring person. Since most feelings are at the subconscious level, they must be analyzed and confessed before their power over us can be broken.

Physical Change

Again, knowing something intellectually or feeling something emotionally doesn't necessarily change anything. We must deliberately avoid the undesirable behavior and substitute new actions for those that need to be deleted. Every time we refrain from the negative response and replace it with the positive response, we strengthen the desired behavior. After about twelve times, the new becomes automatic. Isaiah said, "Cease to do evil; learn to do good" (Isa 1:16–17).

Yes, change is hard, but Jesus said, "For mortals it is impossible, but for God all things are possible" (Matt 19:26).

11: Children Are Different

Each child is valuable, and each child is different. The psalmist said, "Sons are indeed a heritage from the LORD, the fruit of the womb a reward" (Ps 127:3).

Jesus said, "Unless you change and become like children, you will never enter the kingdom of heaven" (Matt 18:3).

Happy and Bubbly Children
They have many friends. They talk a lot and need constant attention. They're wonderful performers, but they tend to act now and think later. It's hard to keep them on task with serious business because they like to have fun. They make excuses and tell tall tales. They need approval and physical affection. To encourage their strengths and avoid their weaknesses, these children need structure, discipline, and organizational skills.

Strong-Willed Children
They are active and bright, but they like to have control. They throw tantrums when they don't get their way. These little bosses are hard to manage, but they also have many strengths. One psychologist said, "The same kid that yells, 'No, I won't do it' to dad at age two will also say, 'No, I won't do it' to the drug dealer at age sixteen."

These children are productive and competent. To encourage their strengths and avoid their weaknesses, they need logical rules and a lot of responsibility.

Children Who Act Like Little Adults
They seem to be four going on forty. These are deep, sensitive, and moody. They want things to be right. They're responsible and perfectionistic. They feel sorry for hungry children and remember hurts for a long time. They may need to be sheltered from violence.

Many of our gifted poets and artists come from this group. They may threaten parents and teachers because they're so different. To encourage their strengths and avoid their weaknesses, these children need to develop positive attitudes and flexible responses.

All-Purpose Children

These children are easygoing and calm. They're never hyperactive or confrontational; unfortunately, they're also world-class procrastinators. Completing homework and cleaning rooms are always going to be done "later." They'll agree and then "forget." They are so passive that they are often neglected.

Nevertheless, they can be very stubborn if pushed too far. To encourage their strengths and avoid their weaknesses, these children need motivation. They must learn how to have initiative and handle conflict.

Each of these personalities must be disciplined in a different way. What will work for one won't work for another. The familiar scripture from Proverbs about rearing children expresses this concept so well: "Train children in the right way, and when old, they will not stray" (see Prov 22:6).

The greatest gift we can give our children is encouraging them to find and follow their own unique path! That's our job as parents, teachers, and mentors. Jesus said, "Let the little children come to me, and do not stop them, for it is to such as these that the kingdom of heaven belongs" (Matt 19:14).

12: Christian Liberty

When the movie *Jonathan Livingston Seagull* was being filmed, the gulls looked as if they had total freedom of movement, but actually they were tied to their perches with almost invisible strings. People are like that. Many individuals look as if they have total freedom. They seem to be rich, famous, successful, and happy. In fact, they are tied by strings of guilt, fear, and resentment. These almost invisible fetters cause the problems in our lives and limit our success.

Normal people want to make their own choices and realize their own dreams. This is a "God-given right." Individuals who feel restrained will eventually become bitter and depressed.

Unfortunately, many religions have added more constraints with rules and moral demands. The Pharisees calculated the exact number of steps you could take on the Sabbath without sinning. They debated whether eating an egg that was laid on the Sabbath was a sin. Jesus was criticized for healing a person on the Sabbath.

Christianity has its own moral dilemmas. A generation ago, dancing was considered to be a sin, but if couples had wheels on their feet, the same action was called skating, and that wasn't a sin. Some churches divide and argue over gender issues, lifestyle choices, and even which political party God prefers. Rules are terrible task masters.

But Jesus abolished such rules. He even broke laws to help people!

Since Paul had suffered under the strict system of rules, he emphasized the liberty of grace, saying, "Now we are discharged from the law, dead to that which held us captive, so that we are enslaved in the newness of the Spirit and not in the oldness of the written code" (Rom 7:6).

Jesus believed in people. He said, "You will know the truth, and the truth will make you free.... If the Son makes you free, you will be free indeed" (John 8:32, 36). He never forced anyone to do his will. He loved the rich young ruler, but he allowed him to walk away.

Jesus yearned for the population of Jerusalem to respond to his message, but he let them make bad choices, saying, "Jerusalem, Jerusalem, the city that kills the prophets and stones those who are sent to it! How often I have desired to gather your children together as a hen gathers her brood under her wings, and you were not willing!" (Matt 23:37).

Nevertheless, many pious individuals actually seek authoritarian leaders. They want to be told exactly what to do. They want "superheroes"! They want reassurance that someone has the answers to life's questions. They want parental figures to lean on. They want experts to tell them what to buy. Under such conditions they'll never mature. Total freedom includes total responsibility, and they are afraid of that.

People who are afraid of liberty may join legalistic cults or vote for strict, dictatorial politicians. They tend to believe shysters, obey mindless creeds, and follow the crowd. They do everything except believe in themselves. Yet the gospel promises that our answers are within. Jesus said, "When the Spirit of truth comes, he will guide you into all the truth" (John 16:13).

The poet Edgar A. Guest wrote,
> The power to choose the work we do,
> To grow and have a larger view,
> To not submit to king or state,
> To be the master of our fate,
> To know, to feel that we are free—
> That is called autonomy!

That is the priceless gift the gospel gives us! Christianity must actually encourage such autonomy.

The Holy Spirit is our internal guidance system. God gave each of us a unique personality and a unique purpose. He gave each of us the freedom to become what we were meant to be. Our Christian walk will look different from everyone else's, and that's okay!

13: A Church Full of Pauls

Every church needs an "Apostle Paul," but it also needs a Barnabas, a Timothy, a Peter, a Thomas, a Martha, and a Mary. Diversity is essential. Paul was a wonderful thinker, organizer, speaker, and writer. These are extremely important roles. Nevertheless, a church full of Pauls would be a disaster because he was also opinionated, egotistical, and quick to judge.

Barnabas, on the other hand, was a mediator, a benefactor, an adviser, and a friend. But a church full of Barnabases would probably be unproductive because he wasn't a strong leader. Timothy was dedicated and helpful, but he was also immature and inexperienced. Peter was earnest but impetuous. Thomas was loyal but skeptical. Martha was hard-working but critical. Mary was intelligent but impractical.

On and on we could go enumerating individual strengths and weaknesses. You see, in churches, as well as in life, diversity is needed. Since no one human being is perfect, each must contribute his or her unique gifts and abilities in order to balance and complete the whole.

Paul explained this clearly with an analogy, saying,

> The body does not consist of one member but of many. If the foot would say, "Because I am not a hand, I do not belong to the body," that would not make it any less a part of the body.... If the whole body were an eye, where would the hearing be? If the whole body were hearing, where would the sense of smell be? But as it is, God arranged the members in the body, each one of them, as he chose.... The eye cannot say to the hand, "I have no need of you," nor again the head to the feet, "I have no need of you." On the contrary, the members of the body that seem to be weaker are indispensable.... The members may have the same care for one another. (see 1 Cor 12:14–15, 17–18, 21–22, 25)

People are different and diversity is essential. If everyone sang solos, there would be no Sunday school teachers. If everyone played the piano, there would be no nursery workers. If everyone preached, there would be no ushers. If everyone counted money and paid bills, there would be no one to cook for dinners, run the vacuum cleaner, or lock the doors. We need many different people with many different talents to be successful.

14: Church Growth

When ministers and religious leaders get together, there's always that inevitable question: "How's your church doing?" Then there's always that equally inevitable reply: "Great! We've raised our budget, doubled our attendance, and started a new building program." This typical evaluation of church growth is known as "nickels and noses." But there are more important ways to evaluate a church. Jesus said, "Where two or three are gathered in my name, I am there among them" (Matt 18:20).

Maybe we should emphasize quality rather than quantity. Instead of finances, attendance, and structures, we should be concerned with intellectual, social, and spiritual matters.

1. *Are we more knowledgeable about the scriptures?* Are we informed about world affairs? Do we emphasize continuing adult education? Are our sermons and lessons relevant and deep?

The writer of Hebrews said, "Everyone who lives on milk, being still an infant, is unskilled in the word of righteousness. But solid food is for the mature, for those whose faculties have been trained by practice to distinguish good from evil" (Heb 5:13–14).

2. *Do we have true harmony in our congregation?* Have we eliminated arrogance, prejudice, and touchiness? Is a spirit of forgiveness and tolerance evident? Are we generous and nonjudgmental? Are we known for our compassion and concern?

Paul said, "Be kind to one another, tenderhearted, forgiving one another" (Eph 4:32).

3. *Are we becoming more Christlike?* Are we guided by the Holy Spirit? Are we free of greed and materialism? Do we feel a "oneness" with others? Does each church member give an accurate reflection of God?

Jesus said, "Be perfect, therefore, as your heavenly Father is perfect" (Matt 5:48).

Of course, it's much harder to evaluate such abstract things than it is to count "nickels and noses." But it's also much more productive and much more scriptural.

15: Common Copouts

When confronted with our faults, failures, and sins, we immediately look for scapegoats. We manufacture alibis. We point fingers. We make excuses. We pass the buck. We rationalize. We justify. We say, "Lord, he made me sin; she made me sin; they made me sin; it made me sin!" We do just about everything except admit our mistakes and take responsibility.

1. *We use our heredity as a loophole.* Many people cop out by claiming a poor heredity. This isn't valid. We aren't determined by our heredity.

We are accountable. An undesirable background can help explain certain difficulties, but it can't be used to escape accountability. So don't blame your heredity. The scripture says, "Parents shall not be put to death for their children, nor shall children be put to death for their parents; only for their own crimes may persons be put to death" (Deut 24:16).

2. *We use our environment as a loophole.* Some people cop out by claiming a wretched environment. None of these excuses is valid. Neither civilization, circumstances, nor associates force us into depravity. We choose!

Each of us must have the courage to do our own thing and be our own person. Of course bad influences and sorry circumstances make it harder for us to achieve, but they can't be used to escape accountability. So don't blame your environment. The scripture says, "You shall not follow a majority in wrongdoing" (Exod 23:2).

3. *We use fate as a loophole.* Some people cop out by claiming that fate is against them. Others say, "The devil made me do it."

Superstition, ill fortune, the odds, and even claiming that tragedies are God's will can all be used to avoid blame. We're like the little boy who, when accused of fighting, pointed to his crying companion and said, "It all started when he hit me back."

We're all sinners. We all fail. We're all weak, ignorant, and lazy. Face yourself. Learn from your mistakes, and go on to better things. Neither your heredity, your environment, nor your fate can keep you down. You are accountable! The scripture says, "Each one of us will be held accountable" (Rom 14:12).

Accepting responsibility is the first step to a new life. If you have problems, if things aren't working out in your family or job, start with yourself. Ask, "What can I do to solve my problem? What can I do to make my marriage better? What can I do to get right with God?"

16: Conceiving, Believing, Achieving

If the mind can conceive it and the heart can believe it, the body can achieve it.

In order to conceive it, we must have the intelligence, the imagination, and the vision to formulate ideas and goals. The writer of Proverbs says, "As he thinketh in his heart, so is he" (Prov 23:7 KJV).

In order to believe it, we must have the confidence, the faith, and the hope to reach for those ideas and goals. Jesus says, "All things can be done for the one who believes" (Mark 9:23).

In order to achieve it, we must have the initiative, the determination, and the persistence to actually accomplish those ideas and goals. Paul says, "Let us not grow weary in doing what it right, for we will reap at harvest time, if we do not give up" (Gal 6:9).

1. *To conceive means to think conceptually.* The thought that leads to no action is not a thought; it's a wish. We must think broader. Don't base your decisions on one side or two sides of an issue when there is an infinite number of sides.

Opposites are not the only options. Two extremes don't average out to perfection. A man with one foot on a hot stove and one foot on a block of ice is not comfortable. The opposite of obesity is starvation, and neither one is desirable. So avoid a seesaw mentality.

We must think deeper: Don't base your conclusions on superficial observations. There is always more than meets the eye. Examine, analyze, and make connections.

We must think longer: Don't base your conclusions on immediate data alone. Realize little mistakes become fatal catastrophes.

Take the long view. Project causes to their logical consequences. Consider all future implications. Ask, "Is this course likely to lead to a dead-end street or an open road?"

Paul says, "We walk by faith, not by sight" (2 Cor 5:7).

2. *To believe means to accept confidently.* A poet wrote,
>You have to believe that the winds will blow.
>Believe there'll be grass while watching the snow.

And that's the reason the bird can sing.
On gloomy, dark days, he believes in spring.

Miracles come from faith. Jesus said, "Whatever you ask for in prayer with faith, you will receive" (Matt 21:22).

First, there is faith in ourselves. We must have self-respect and self-confidence.

Second, there is faith in others. We must rely on our support group and expect the best from those around us.

Third, there is faith in God. We must believe that universal principles are on the side of truth and righteousness. Jesus said, "If you have faith the size of a mustard seed, you will say to this mountain, 'Move from here to there,' and it will move, and nothing will be impossible for you" (Matt 17:20).

3. To achieve means to act productively. Two children stood looking out the window at a rainbow. Suddenly, the older boy made a smug pronouncement, "God makes rainbows! God makes everything!"

"Well," his little brother replied with a sad glance at their rumpled, disorganized room, "God sure don't make beds!"

This casual observation expresses a deep theological principle. Why does God make rainbows but not beds? Why does God make mountains but not skyscrapers? Why does God make oceans but not bathtubs?

You see, we can't create worlds and universes and natural resources, but we can make beds. It's obvious that God's part stops where ours begins. We must make our own beds!

"Faith is the assurance of things hoped for, the conviction of things not seen" (Heb 11:1).

What you can conceive and believe, you can achieve.

17: Could I? Should I? Would I?

Jesus didn't try to do everything. He had the same time, energy, and resource constraints that we do. He didn't solve every problem. He didn't cure every disease. He didn't feed every beggar.

Instead, he responded to those issues that represented the best use of his special abilities. That's what we must do. Every day, we confront situations that demand our attention. Since we can't do everything, when we do see a problem, we must ask ourselves three important questions: "Could I do this? Should I do this? Would I do this?"

Solomon said, "Do not withhold good from those to whom it is due, when it is in your power to do it" (Prov 3:27). He knew that no one is able to help everyone with every problem. Paul said, "Each has a particular gift from God, one having one kind and another a different kind" (1 Cor 7:7).

People are responsible for using the special abilities they've been given.

1. *Asking "Could I do this?" means "Is this possible?"* If we're asked to go to Mars, we know that's not possible at this time. So the decision is already made for us.

If I'm asked to sail a ship across the desert, we know the resources are not available for that since there's no water to float a boat. So I can check that off.

But what if I'm expected to run a marathon? Well, that's possible. It's been done many times. The resources are available. But if I've never trained to race and if I have a bad knee, I'm not capable of successfully completing a marathon. So the answer to "Could I do this?" is "No!"

If I'm asked to bake cookies for a church social, then that is possible. The resources are available. I have flour, sugar, spices, and an oven. So the answer to the question "Could I do this?" is "Yes!"

At this point we must ask the next question: "Should I do this?"

Solomon said, "Even children make themselves known by their acts" (Prov 20:11).

Not every action is necessary or moral. Some things need to be left alone. Some situations will work themselves out.

2. *Asking "Should I do this?" means "Is this necessary and productive?"* Do we really need these cookies? Am I the best baker available? Would it be difficult to get some other person to accept this task?

Then we must find out if the activity is productive. Will it help other people or fill a real need? If cookies will attract young people to an inspirational service, then the answer is "Yes!"

If, after examining the situation, we realize that this is a productive activity, cookies are needed, and we're the most logical person to provide them, then we must move to the last and most personal question: Would I do this?

Solomon said, "Whatever your hand finds to do, do with your might" (Eccl 9:10).

3. *Asking "Would I do this?" means "Is this something worthwhile for me to do now?"* Is it practical, considering my special talents and energy and time constraints? Is my motivation to respond from an honest desire to serve? Do I have enough skills and interest to persevere and finish the task successfully?

Many people begin projects and then bail out before they're finished. So these three questions are crucial in decision-making: Could I? Should I? Would I?

Paul said, "See that you complete the task that you have received in the Lord" (Col 4:17).

18: Cutting Out the Middleman

When customers buy from farmers at the public market, they are cutting out the middleman. When businessmen go directly to the manufacturers for a wholesale deal, they are cutting out the middleman. Most economists feel this is good. When consumers are separated from production sources, price gouging results. Middlemen can always prey on the ignorance of the uninformed.

From primitive times, individuals have felt separated from their divine source. The fear, loneliness, and helplessness inherent in this condition caused feelings of alienation.

Shrewd priests, witch doctors, and medicine men have always capitalized on the ignorance and anxieties of the uninformed. People have been taught that they must go through channels to reach and influence the gods. These channels included religious leaders, elaborate ceremonies, prescribed rituals, proper sacrifices, and generous offerings. The "separation syndrome" was symbolized and perpetuated by walls, barriers, veils, mysteries, and taboos.

The temple rulers and anointed holy ones were the middlemen. These agents claimed to mediate between the average person and his god. In reality, individuals were often at the mercy of unscrupulous and manipulative dictators who used religion to enslave and rob.

Under this system there was little hope of personal growth. There was little chance of autonomy. There were few opportunities for spiritual development.

Before mankind could be really human, in the fullest, most responsible sense, something had to change! Unfortunately, change is difficult. Conditioning and customs are powerful. The bonds of superstition are strong.

Reconciliation was one important purpose of Jesus's incarnation. He became the link between God and mankind. That's why the priests and scribes hated him.

The religious teachers were threatened when Jesus said, "God is spirit, and those who worship him must worship in spirit and truth," not necessarily in temples (John 4:24).

Many religious leaders of our day are also threatened when we teach that God wants us to be independent discoverers of truth instead of obedient followers of authority. Only the middlemen expect to gain by our ignorance. Only doctrinal dictators want us to swallow every line. Only evangelistic hucksters want us to buy their spiritual snake oil! Don't believe them!

Jesus lived and died to cut out the middleman! He did not even allow his followers to make him a permanent middleman. He said, "I do not say to you that I will ask the Father on your behalf, for the Father himself loves you" (John 16:26–27).

We can go to God ourselves! We don't need earthly middlemen!

19: Don't Blame Me

"I'm not guilty! I'm not guilty! I'm not guilty!"

Ducking responsibility is a universal game. Every criminal trial is an exercise in denial.

1. *I didn't do it.* The perpetrator says, "I'm not guilty because I didn't do it." He tries to establish alibis to prove that he couldn't possible have been at that place at that time. He bribes witnesses to substantiate his claim of innocence. If that doesn't work, he moves on to another level of denial.

2. *They made me do it.* The perpetrator says, "I'm not guilty because they made me do it." He cites peer pressure. He says, "Others did worse." The gang, the organization, or the situation forced me to act as I did. He tries to convince everyone that he was compelled to do what he did. If that doesn't work, he moves on to the last level of denial.

3. *I couldn't help it.* The perpetrator says, "I'm not guilty because even if I did it and even if they didn't make me do it, I'm still not guilty because I couldn't help it."

He says, "I was temporarily insane." "I was mentally impaired." "I was under the influence of alcohol." "I was in such an emotional state that I just couldn't control myself."

Is anyone ever guilty of his crime? Is anyone ever responsible for his actions? Is anyone ever to blame for his evil deeds?

In an old story, a governor visited a prison. As he talked to each inmate, he heard the same excuses: "Oh, Governor, I'm innocent." "They arrested the wrong man." "I got a raw deal." "The judge had it in for me."

Over and over, every man denied and excused his behavior. At last, one lone fellow said, "Yeah, Governor, I'm guilty. I did it. No one forced me. I'm responsible. I knew better, and now I'm sorry."

The governor immediately ordered the man released, saying, "I can't have this terrible sinner in here with all these poor, innocent men. He'll contaminate them."

Are we in denial? Do we blame others for our faults? Do we justify our behavior? The world will never improve until individuals get beyond denial and become responsible. That's what repentance and confession are all about. The scripture says, "If we say that we have no sin, we deceive ourselves, and the truth is not in us. If we confess our sins, he who is faithful and just will forgive us our sins and cleanse us from all unrighteousness. If we say that we have not sinned, we make him a liar, and his word is not in us" (1 John 1:8–10).

20: Down but Not Out!

It's paradoxical that the worst can often become the best. God often used troublemakers.

Moses was high-tempered, argumentative, and stubborn, but after Moses killed a man, he met God at the burning bush (see Exod 3:2ff).

Jacob was deceitful, selfish, and scheming, but after Jacob was exiled in disgrace, he had a vision at Bethel (see Gen 28:10–22).

Joseph was arrogant, boastful, and egotistical, but after Joseph was sold into Egyptian slavery, he learned to forgive and serve (see Gen 45).

Peter was headstrong, impetuous, and undisciplined, but after Peter cursed and denied the Lord, he was empowered to preach at Pentecost (see Acts 2).

Paul was aggressive, intolerant, and vindictive, but after Paul sanctioned the stoning of Stephen, he was commissioned as a missionary on the road to Damascus (see Acts 9).

Yes, troublemakers have potential. Sometimes it's easier to channel and tone down an energetic maverick than it is to motivate an indolent loafer. Abraham Lincoln said, "It's obvious that folks with no vices have few virtues!"

At least the troublemakers have initiative and determination. These crucial traits don't have to be developed. They only have to be disciplined! Also, it's often out of our failures that we grow.

All of us have weaknesses and make mistakes. It's how we react to them that determines our future.

The gospel helps us realize that God can use troublemakers. It says that it's our future, not our past, that's important. It assures us that the worst can often become the best.

21: The Edge of the Unknown

Today we stand on the edge of the unknown. A new year stretches before us. We don't know what changes it will bring. We don't know what problems will confront us. We don't know what trials we'll have to deal with.

Once, when the Israelites faced unknown territory, they received the following reassurance: "The eyes of the LORD your God are always on it, from the beginning of the year to the end of the year" (Deut 11:12).

Then, later, when these Israelites stood at a crossroads that required a courageous decision, the scriptures give these instructions: "When you see the ark of the covenant of the LORD…you shall set out from your place. Follow it, so that you may know the way you should go, for you have not passed this way before" (see Josh 3:3–4).

The ark symbolized God's presence and guidance. So following the ark meant following the Lord.

At this moment, when one year ends and another begins, we too stand at a crossroads. We too have never been this way before. Our future is unexplored. We don't know what lies ahead globally, nationally, or personally.

At the new year we need to take a spiritual inventory. We need to get a moral checkup. Our strengths, our weaknesses, and our growth must be evaluated. We must make resolutions. Then we must fulfill our vows and keep our promises.

Ask yourself: What attitudes need to be changed? What forgiveness needs to be extended? What relationships need to be restored? What habits need to be broken? What discipline needs to be established?

Today we stand on the edge of the unknown. We don't know what the new year will bring. But remember, "the Lord our God will care for us from the beginning of the year to the end of the year."

22: Emotional Paupers

Let's imagine two dogs: One is a mongrel with no master and no home. He's never seen Alpo or Gravy Train. In fact, he hasn't eaten anything for a week. Suddenly, he spies a juicy bone. Just as he clamps it between his jaws, a rival stray lunges toward him and tries to take it.

Another imaginary dog is a pampered poodle. He has a home and a collar. He eats three meals a day plus dog "yummies." In fact, he's even allowed to eat steak from his master's plate. Today, however, the poodle also finds a bone on the street. As he sniffs the morsel, a stray tries to take it.

Which dog would feel more threatened by this attack? Which dog would be more devastated by the loss? Which dog would fight harder to retain his bone? The one who had less to begin with, of course. A dog with plenty of food would not be as upset by a small loss as the dog who had very little.

Now let's imagine two men: The first one is almost destitute. He has no property, no checking account, and no credit cards. He is alone on the streets of a strange city—tired, cold, and afraid. Suddenly, he sees a sign: "Rooms for the night, $5." This man has one five-dollar bill in his pocket. With a sigh of relief, he hurries toward the safety and warmth of the rooming house. Just then a mugger accosts him and tries to take his money.

Another imaginary man is a millionaire with homes, yachts, and limousines. He too walks down the street. He too meets a mugger who accosts him and tries to take his money.

Which man will feel more threatened by this attack? Which man would be more devastated by the loss? Which man would fight harder to retain his money? The one who had less to begin with, of course! A man with plenty of money would not be as defensive or upset by a small loss as the man who had very little!

Now let's compare two individuals: Both are verbally accosted by an associate. Both are snubbed and criticized.

Which one would feel more threatened by the attack? Which one would be more devastated by the "loss of face"? Which one would fight harder to retain his self-image? The one who has less to begin with, of course. In other words, an individual with plenty of self-esteem, personal assurance, and inner confidence will not be as upset by a small snub as the individual who had little self-esteem, assurance, and confidence!

Therefore, when you see a person with a "chip on his shoulder," when you see a person with his "feelings on his sleeve," when you see a person who "takes everything the wrong way," when you see a person who is constantly defensive, you know you are observing an "emotional pauper."

A person who is secure in his role as God's child—in short, a "spiritual millionaire"—will be able to sustain small losses of esteem with a minimum of emotional damage and therefore with a minimum of destructive reaction.

People of faith have strength and spiritual support. They rely on God's love and protection. The psalmist says, "It is better to take refuge in the LORD than to put confidence in mortals" (Ps 118:8).

Paul says, "Your faith might rest not on human wisdom but on the power of God" (1 Cor 2:5).

23: Excuses, Excuses, Excuses!

Excuses are needed, we all would agree—
They let me blame you and exonerate me!

Yes, we blame others. We point fingers. We use distractions. We justify. We rationalize. We manufacture alibis. We claim our exemptions. In short, most of us will do just about anything to avoid responsibility.

The Blame Game

Adam passed the buck. He did a weak and stupid thing. He let others think for him. Then, when confronted with his misdeed, he denied his responsibility and pointed his finger at Eve. Eve, in turn, denied her responsibility and pointed her finger at the snake. And then, as a comic remarked, "The snake didn't have a leg to stand on."

We project our own deficiencies onto those around us. When rats in a lab are shocked, they can't retaliate against the scientist, so they attack the nearest rat. The man who can't hit his boss hits his wife. The woman who can't scream at the policeman yells at her children.

The alternative to the "blame game" is to accept responsibility, admit your weaknesses, remedy your mistakes, and get beyond your failures.

The Pity Party Ploy

Elijah was tired. He had been burning his candle at both ends. He was afraid and under pressure. His showdown with the false prophets was over, and he'd won, but the letdown and depression continued. After a long day Elijah collapsed under a tree, saying, "Poor me. I'm the only good person left. I'm the only one who cares about life's problems. I'm the only one who's faithful. The world can't run without me." These symptoms often attack the busiest and most dedicated leaders when they're overworked and near burnout!

The alternative to the "pity party ploy" is to get some rest, nourishment, and a new perspective.

The Clean Hands Complex

When Pilate saw that he was getting nowhere, but that instead the crowd was restless and an uproar was starting, he took water and washed his hands in front of the crowd and said, "I am innocent of this man's blood. It is your responsibility!"

Pilate wanted to please the public and save his own neck.

We also try to avoid trouble by keeping our hands clean. An old adage says, "Success has a thousand fathers, but failure is an orphan."

The alternative to the "clean hands complex" is to make the right choices or correct your wrong choices and then accept the responsibility for your actions.

None of these excuses work. The scripture says, "If we willfully persist in sin after having received the knowledge of the truth, there no longer remains a sacrifice for sins" (Heb 10:26).

24: Failure Is Not Final!

From childhood on we've been told, "Don't be a quitter!" "Keep on keeping on!" "Never give up!" "If at first you don't succeed, try, try again!"

Tenacity, persistence, and determination—that's what made America great! Success, victory, and winning. Success, victory, and winning are the buzz words.

So what did Jesus mean when he said, "If anyone will not welcome you or listen to your words, shake off the dust from your feet as you leave that house or town" (Matt 10:14). Does this mean we're not to go back again and again? We're not to beg and plead and wring our hands? We're not to blame ourselves and resolve to do better?

As usual the Lord creates a paradox.

An early theologian calls this text "the forgotten commandment," "the doctrine of failure." Why did Jesus feel this admonition was necessary? Why is it repeated in three of the Gospels?

Jesus knew we would fail! In fact, he had experienced failure himself! His neighbors in Nazareth rejected him; the rich young ruler walked away; the citizens of Jerusalem condemned him.

But Jesus also knew something else: He knew that failure isn't final. You can lose every battle and still win the war. He knew that if you don't fail occasionally, you're not really trying. He knew that if you're afraid to fail, you won't risk! He knew it's "better to fail in a good cause than to succeed in a bad one"! That's why he gave instructions for constructive failure.

His statement is simple and positive. He recommended that we have no useless regrets, no second-guessing, no crying over spilt milk. He was saying, "Just share the honest message of your heart, and if you meet no response, move on!

"Shake off the dust from your feet." These are tough words. They seem to contradict the current motivational principles. Yet Jesus gave this clear, specific command to his followers.

This scripture tells us that we are not indispensable in the scheme of things. There are other methods and other voices. If my ministry is not successful, maybe someone else's will be. It's a team effort.

It reassures us that when things don't work out, we are not necessarily guilty. Those crushing defeats may not be our fault. There are many complex elements in life. If we do our best and it's not good enough, the cause may be something beyond our control. God understands!

It reminds us that God doesn't nag! He respects people's autonomy! We can't fix the world. Even Jesus couldn't fix the world! Free will is absolute! After we've done our part, the responsibility is squarely on the hearer.

It explains that our time and energy are limited. There are many fields of service. There are other fish in the sea. It's neither wise nor effective to waste all our energy in one spot.

This principle proves that some causes are not worth our efforts. It's useless to "throw your pearls before swine" (see Matt 7:6).

So to "shake off the dust from your feet" means that if you give a relationship or a project your best shot and it isn't successful, don't worry. God loves you anyway. Furthermore, the kingdom will not fail because of one setback. Shake it off, leave it behind, and go on.

25: Faith Needs Feet

Faith is essential and powerful, but faith has its limitations. James says you can't eat it or wear it or spend it: "What good is it, my brothers and sisters, if someone claims to have faith but does not have works? Surely that faith cannot save, can it? If a brother or sister is naked and lacks daily food and one of you says to them, 'Go in peace; keep warm and eat your fill,' and yet you do not supply their bodily needs, what is the good of that? So faith by itself, if it has no works, is dead" (see Jas 2:14–17).

In fact, most of the scriptural terms for faith mean "faithfulness" rather than wishful thinking or hopeful feelings. Faith is a lifestyle! "'The righteous live by their faithfulness" (Hab 2:4).

The Hebrew word translated *faith* means "being trustworthy."

This practical definition is used in Jesus's statement, "Well done, good and trustworthy slave; you have been trustworthy in a few things; I will put you in charge of many things" (Matt 25:23).

It explains John's statement, "Be faithful until death, and I will give you the crown of life" (Rev 2:10).

Faith includes a mental outlook, but its flip side, "feet," is the positive action. "Wishes won't wash dishes," and "faith won't pay bills." James explained this clearly, saying, "Someone will say, 'You have faith, and I have works.' Show me your faith apart from your works, and I by my works will show you faith" (Jas 2:18).

Misconceptions in this area abound. Many sincere Christians think holding an unrealistic expectation is faith. Many sincere Christians think God wants us to depend upon divine miracles instead of human energy. Many sincere Christians think supernatural inspiration can replace natural perspiration.

Such beliefs are neither scriptural nor reasonable.

Paul equates faith with confidence: "We are always confident...for we walk by faith, not by sight. Yes, we do have confidence" (2 Cor 5:6–8).

The writer of Hebrews equates faith with initiative: "Faith is the assurance of things hoped for, the conviction of things not seen" (Heb 11:1).

James equates faith with determination: "Faith was active along with his works, and by works faith was brought to completion" (Jas 2:22).

Faith needs feet!

26: Five Rules for Living

1. Quit worrying about things that don't matter! If you have a bad hair day or a burned toast day, it doesn't matter. Suppose an acquaintance fails to speak to you or your boss frowns at you. It doesn't matter. Suppose you catch every red light and a slow car gets ahead of you. Well, a year from now, or even a week from now, you won't even remember that, so it doesn't matter! Paul said, "Do not be anxious about anything, but in everything by prayer and supplication with thanksgiving let your requests be made known to God" (Phil 4:6).

2. Realize that others are not thinking about you! You may believe your friends are contemplating your virtues and your enemies are enumerating your vices. They aren't! You're sure the postman, your mother-in-law, and the stranger on the street all noticed the five pounds you've gained. They didn't! You just know everyone you meet is discussing your aging body and your failing mind. Instead, those people are all thinking about their own problems, just like you are! Paul said, "Each one of us will be held accountable" (Rom 14:12).

3. Develop your strengths instead of correcting your weaknesses. A fish will never be a great runner, and a rabbit will never be a great climber, and you'll never be a great opera star if you're tone deaf. Don't waste time on unproductive projects. Go with your strengths and folks won't notice your weaknesses! Paul said, "Do not neglect the gift that is in you" (1 Tim 4:14).

4. Eliminate the word *later* from your vocabulary. It's easy to see a job that needs to be done and say, "I'll do it later." You won't! It's tempting to buy an extravagant item and say, "I'll pay for this later." You can't! Saying "I'll study later; I'll clean up later; I'll exercise later" merely alleviates your present guilt. It accomplishes nothing, because "later" never becomes "now." The scripture says, "Whatever your hand finds to do, do with your might, for there is no work or thought or knowledge or wisdom in [the grave]" (Eccl 9:10).

5. Don't express your "constructive criticisms." If your friend has a behavior flaw that's really obvious, you may think a word of wisdom will set

them straight and they'll be grateful. They won't! You think pointing out a colleague's faults will cause them to reform on the spot. It won't! You think your loved ones will appreciate you for "helping" them overcome their bad attitudes. They won't! So if you value your relationships, forget criticism! Jesus said, "Do not judge, so that you may not be judged" (Matt 7:1).

If we all followed these five rules, we would be obeying Jesus's admonition when he said, "Blessed are the peacemakers, for they will be called children of God" (Matt 5:9).

27: Five Steps to Faith

The scripture says, "The one who is righteous will live by faith" (Gal 3:11).

The Christian gospel is based upon the power of faith. Science is discovering why this principle is so important. Expecting a particular outcome does something in our brains. If you expect a medicine to work, it often will, even if it's only a sugar pill. In one study, when participants drank wine they'd been told was expensive, the part of their brains that registers pleasure lit up more than when they drank wine they'd been told was "cheap," even though it was the same wine.

Studies show that what we believe can actually change the structure of our brains. Scientists call this neuroplasticity.

Surprisingly, both psychology and the Bible tell us that these five principles are important for a successful project.

1. *Analyze it.* You must have an attainable goal. Saying "I'm becoming financially secure" will be more effective than saying "I am becoming a billionaire" because it's more reasonable. Paul said, "Hope that is seen is not hope, for who hopes for what one already sees? But if we hope for what we do not see, we wait for it with patience" (Rom 8:24–25).

2. *Desire it.* You must be totally sincere. It must be a deep, heartfelt yearning, not a passing fancy. God said, "When you search for me, you will find me; if you seek me with all your heart" (Jer 29:13).

3. *Believe it.* You must avoid doubt! You have to believe it's possible. Disbelief will negate the affirmation. James said, "Ask in faith, never doubting, for the one who doubts is like a wave of the sea, driven and tossed by the wind. For the doubter, being double-minded and unstable in every way, must not expect to receive anything from the Lord" (Jas 1:6–7).

4. *Visualize it.* You must picture it vividly. Sports psychologists use mental imagery to enhance performance. The brain can't differentiate between simulation and actuality. As you focus on your affirmation, try to see and feel it happening. The scripture says, "Faith is the assurance of things hoped for, the conviction of things not seen" (Heb 11:1).

5. *Express it.* You must use statements that are short, simple, and positive. Say "I'm happy" rather than "I'm not upset." If you think in the negative, you are placing your emphasis on what's wrong rather than what's right. Saying your affirmation out loud implies a commitment that makes it more likely you'll take the necessary actions to reach your goal. Paul said, "For one believes with the heart, leading to righteousness, and one confesses with the mouth, leading to salvation" (Rom 10:10).

28: Fixers and Fanatics?

What really drives those fanatical crusaders who are out to fix everyone and make over the world? Is it genuine concern? Are they trying to benefit those they criticize? Do they have a deep desire to increase the well-being of mankind?

No! No! And no!

A person who is rigid and intolerant has one of three basic motives:

Arrogance

Proving that "I'm right and you're wrong" boosts my ego. Putting others down makes me feel "up." Criticizing others makes me look better. So I pray the Pharisee's prayer: "God, I thank you that I am not like other people" (Luke 18:11).

Control

Being in charge can be addictive. I begin to think it's my mission in life to make others conform to my image. I decide that I have the right to force those around me to believe as I do and to behave as I wish. Jesus warned against this attitude, saying, "Why do you see the speck in your neighbor's eye but do not notice the log in your own eye? Or how can you say to your neighbor, 'Let me take the speck out of your eye,' while the log is in your own eye?" (Matt 7:3–4).

Security

There is safety in numbers, so if many others agree with me, then I can convince myself that my way is best. I can't just "live and let live" because diverse opinions threaten my own sense of certainty.

Jesus never used these tactics. He never coerced anyone. He allowed people to believe and say and do what they pleased. He even allowed the rich young ruler to walk away (see Mark 10:21–22).

Over and over, he told his disciples to leave others alone. When his followers criticized a group who was using his name, Jesus refused to forbid them, saying, "Do not stop him…. Whoever is not against us is for us" (Mark 9:39–40).

When Martha tried to boss Mary, Jesus rebuked her, saying, "Martha, Martha, you are worried and distracted by many things, but few things are needed—indeed only one. Mary has chosen the better part, which will not be taken away from her" (Luke 10:41–42).

When Peter was nosy about a fellow apostle's future plans and asked, "Lord, what about him?," Jesus told him it was none of his business, saying, "If it is my will that he remain until I come, what is that to you? Follow me!" (John 21:21–22).

In one of his stories about the enemy who sowed tares among the wheat, Jesus made a point of non-interference: "The slaves said to him, 'Then do you want us to go and gather them?' But he replied, 'No, for in gathering the weeds you would uproot the wheat along with them. Let both of them grow together until the harvest'" (see Matt 13:28–30).

So beware of fanatical do-gooders.

29: Forgiveness

We are such insecure, defensive, and hostile creatures that self-protection becomes a conditioned reflex, and blaming others becomes a way of life. Since all of us experience pain and rejection, all of us have animosities. Therefore, all of us must deal with the problem of forgiveness. Unfortunately, forgiveness is not easy. In fact, if it's offered too readily, it's probably not honest. True forgiveness involves a process.

1. *We hurt!* This is the normal human response to an injury or slight. We must feel it and analyze it. We must not deny it or minimize it. The hurt is real and deep. It happened, and it matters. Jesus said this would happen: "They will hand you over to be tortured and will put you to death, and you will be hated by all nations because of my name" (Matt 24:9).

2. *We hide!* This stage is almost inevitable, but it's totally unproductive. Repression may "fix" things for the moment, but the resentments aren't dead. Instead, they are buried alive and subject to resurrection at the most inopportune moments. Jesus said, "Nothing is covered up that will not be uncovered and nothing secret that will not become known" (Luke 12:2).

3. *We hate!* Anger is a natural instinct, and most normal human beings seek revenge. We want to retaliate. An "eye for an eye" is merely the outward expression of the inner hostility. It's this stage of fury that requires the greatest measure of God's grace. Paul said, "Never avenge yourselves…for it is written, 'Vengeance is mine; I will repay,' says the Lord" (Rom 12:19).

4. *We heal!* A full understanding of our "enemy" and his problems, plus a humble assessment of our own weaknesses and limitations, can help us let go of our bitterness. This leads to inner peace. God helps us in this process. The psalmist said, "He heals the brokenhearted and binds up their wounds" (Ps 147:3).

5. *We help!* After we feel our hurt, admit our resentments, rise above our hatred, and experience healing, then and only then can we help others. Paul said, "Bless those who persecute you; bless and do not curse them" (Rom 12:14).

Those who have been forgiven can forgive! Those who forgive can be forgiven! That's the spiritual paradox.

30: Forgive Their Ignorance

When Jesus was being crucified, he looked at his murderers and said, "Father, forgive them, for they do not know what they are doing" (Luke 23:34).

Now, he was not being soft on sin, and he was certainly not excusing personal responsibility. Instead, he was expressing a valid psychological principle. He knew that most evil is done in ignorance.

Later, Peter expressed this same thing to a crowd of people: "The God of our ancestors, has glorified his servant Jesus, whom you handed over and rejected in the presence of Pilate, though he had decided to release him. But you rejected the holy and righteous one and asked to have a murderer given to you, and you killed the author of life, whom God raised from the dead. To this we are witnesses.... Now, brothers and sisters, I know that you acted in ignorance, as did also your rulers" (Acts 3:13–15, 17).

Ignorance is a great sin. It promotes fear, and fear promotes defensiveness; defensiveness promotes hostility, and hostility promotes violence.

When you are attacked by someone, say to yourself, "This person is probably feeling very threatened and insecure." Then you can choose to respond in one of three ways:

1. *If the offense is slight and general:* Ignore situations that include yelling and negativity. Instead, be attentive when the discussion is reasonable and positive.

2. *If the offense is occasional and impersonal:* Say, "I'm sorry you are upset." Ask, "Is there anything I can do to make you feel better?"

3. *If the offense is extreme, often, and personal:* You may need to become assertive. Use "I" language and say, "I do not appreciate your comments. Please speak to me in a respectful manner."

If these don't work, try to avoid the offensive individual. That was Jesus's advice to his disciples. He said, "Do not give what is holy to dogs, and do not throw your pearls before swine, or they will trample them under foot and turn and maul you" (Matt 7:6).

"If anyone will not welcome you or listen to your words, shake off the dust from your feet as you leave that house or town" (Matt 10:14).

31: Four Basic Needs

The Bible says Jesus grew in four normal ways (see Luke 2:52). These four areas define the basic human needs:

1. *We need to live!* The survival instinct is essential. We must have food, clothing, shelter, and protection from danger. If these needs are not met, nothing else matters. Jesus grew in years and size. This means that he grew physically.

2. *We need to love!* We must belong to a family and a community. We long for connection with others. Acceptance, approval, and appreciation from our friends are important. Jesus grew in favor with mankind. This means he grew socially!

3. *We need to learn!* Our minds are as hungry as our bodies. We're made to think and develop intellectually. Information, knowledge, and education feed us. Jesus grew and increased in wisdom. This means he grew mentally!

4. *We need to leave a legacy!* We must have purpose and meaning. We are here to make a contribution. Fulfilling this need gives us permanence and satisfaction. Jesus grew in favor with God. This means he grew spiritually!

These four areas must balance. If these needs are unmet, addictions often occur because we try to fill the emptiness with artificial substitutes like drugs, alcohol, money, sex, shopping, or excitement. So let's live, love, learn, and leave a legacy!

32: Giving for the Right Reason

We've all heard the scripture, "It is more blessed to give than to receive" (Acts 20:35). Unfortunately, some giving is not blessed because it's given for the wrong reason.

1. *Some give to receive praise.* They want to look good before their neighbors, but Jesus said, "Beware of practicing your righteousness before others in order to be seen by them, for then you have no reward from your Father in heaven. So whenever you give alms, do not sound a trumpet before you, as the hypocrites do" (Matt 6:1–2).

2. *Others give to feel superior.* When they take food or clothing to soup kitchens and thrift stores, the subtle message may be, "I'm rich and successful. You people are poor failures." But Paul said, "Do nothing from selfish ambition or conceit, but in humility regard others as better than yourselves" (Phil 2:3).

3. *Controllers give as a trade or a bribe.* "I'll give if you will return the favor by doing what I want you to do." In other words, "Remember, you're obligated to me." But Jesus said, "If you do good to those who do good to you, what credit is that to you? For even sinners do the same. If you lend to those from whom you hope to receive payment, what credit is that to you? Even sinners lend to sinners, to receive as much again" (Luke 6:33–34).

4. *Many people give to relieve their own guilt.* Instead of sharing themselves, they give material things. But Paul said, "If I give away all my possessions and if I hand over my body so that I may boast but do not have love, I gain nothing" (1 Cor 13:3).

5. *We may give out of custom or habit.* No thought or feeling accompanies this gift. We just do our duty because we've always done it. But Paul said, "Each of you must give as you have made up your mind, not regretfully or under compulsion, for God loves a cheerful giver" (2 Cor 9:7).

As Christians, let's give for the right reason, with joy and with no strings attached. "You received without payment; give without payment" (Matt 10:8).

33: God Knows Your Name

A professor explained to his class of student nurses that they would meet and serve many individuals. He said, "All of them are significant. They are not anonymous robots. They need your attention and care. They deserve to hear you speak their names."

Our name is important to us. It picks us out of the crowd. It acknowledges our special qualities.

The scriptures say God does indeed know our name. In almost every spiritual encounter, the person is touched and changed when God calls them by name.

Moses

The scriptures say, "God called to him out of the bush, 'Moses, Moses!' And he said, 'Here I am'" (Exod 3:4).

Then God informed him that this was a personal message. Being singled out by name makes us individually responsible. We can't say, "Let someone else do it" or "I'm just one of the crowd" or "It's not my job."

When Moses was confronted with his moment of truth, he was told what to do, and he became accountable for his actions.

Samuel

The scriptures say, "The LORD came and stood there, calling as before, 'Samuel! Samuel!' And Samuel said, 'Speak, for your servant is listening.'… As Samuel grew up, the Lord was with him" (1 Sam 3:10, 19).

Samuel heard a voice and woke up from drowsiness and sleep to inquire about it. Then God gave him a personal message. Again, being singled out by name makes us individually responsible.

Paul

The scriptures say, "Saul, still breathing threats and murder against the disciples of the Lord, went to the high priest and asked him for letters to the synagogues at Damascus, so that if he found any who belonged to the Way, men or women, he might bring them bound to Jerusalem. Now as he was going along and approaching Damascus, suddenly a light from heaven flashed around him. He fell to the ground and heard a voice saying to him, 'Saul, Saul, why do you persecute me?' He asked, 'Who are you, Lord?' The reply came, 'I am Jesus, whom you are persecuting. But get up and enter the city, and you will be told what you are to do'" (Acts 9:1–6).

Later, his mission was clearly defined. God said, "'[Saul] is an instrument whom I have chosen to bring my name before gentiles and kings and before the people of Israel.'... And immediately he began to proclaim Jesus in the synagogues, saying, 'He is the Son of God'" (Acts 9:15, 20).

This isn't a strange accident. It's a personal message. Being singled out by name makes us individually responsible. It changed this man's identity from "murderer" to "missionary."

A wise man said, "There are many people who can do the big things, but there are few people who are willing to do the small things. Yet, the small things must be done."

God knows our name. God is calling us by name. Have we responded?

34: God's Plan for You

You are not an accident! Your life has a purpose. The scripture says, "'I know the plans I have for you,' says the LORD, 'plans for your welfare and not for harm, to give you a future with hope'" (Jer 29:11).

Until you discover that plan and adapt your behavior to follow that plan, you'll be unhappy and unsuccessful. At the end of your life, you'll be evaluated according to how closely you have followed that plan. Every decision you make, every word you speak, and every deed you do is important in the grand scheme of things. They will either keep you closer to that plan or move you further away from that plan.

1. *God's plan for you is personal, not generic.* God designed it specifically for you. It's individualized and different from every other person's plan.

No two people are alike. Christians are not "cookie-cutter saints." Peter was nothing like John. Paul was nothing like Barnabas, yet we're all reflections of God.

Paul said, "The body does not consist of one member but of many. If the foot would say, 'Because I am not a hand, I do not belong to the body,' that would not make it any less a part of the body. And if the ear would say, 'Because I am not an eye, I do not belong to the body,' that would not make it any less a part of the body. If the whole body were an eye, where would the hearing be? If the whole body were hearing, where would the sense of smell be?" (1 Cor 12:14–17).

In other words, each one of us is important. God's plan for you may be entirely different from his plan for your relatives and friends. No two pieces of a jigsaw puzzle are exactly alike, and no two Christians are exactly alike.

2. *God's plan for you is good, not evil.* God wants what's best for you. God never sends evil into your life. He is not the author of tragedy. Bad things may happen, but God doesn't cause them. Rather, he can help you overcome the problems and even use them for good.

Paul said, "We know that all things work together for good for those who love God, who are called according to his purpose" (Rom 8:28).

We can safely and confidently say, "Your will be done," because we know his will is perfect for us.

3. *God's plan for you includes hope, not despair.* It leads to success, not failure. Things may not seem to be pleasant or successful in the short term, but God sees the future. He has the overall view, and you can trust that he is working for your ultimate well-being over the long term.

When you are following God's plan, you are "in the groove." You are fulfilled; projects get done; relationships are peaceful. When you deviate from God's plan, the opposite happens. You are unfulfilled; projects don't get done; relationships become hostile.

Paul ignored this principle in his early years. God had an important plan for him, but he chose a destructive path. The scripture says, "He fell to the ground and heard a voice saying to him, 'Saul, Saul, why do you persecute me?' He asked, 'Who are you, Lord?' The reply came, 'I am Jesus, whom you are persecuting. But get up and enter the city, and you will be told what you are to do'" (Acts 9:4–6).

Fortunately, Paul obeyed, and when he got in sync with God's plan, we know what a great life he had and what wonderful things he accomplished.

Discover God's plan for you through prayer, Bible study, good advice, and common sense. Stop a moment to repeat this promise:

> Today, I face a future with paths I cannot see,
> But still I vow to follow God's special plan for me!"
> —Maralene Wesner

35: The Gospel in a Nutshell

Jesus seldom answered questions directly. Instead, he usually asked another question or told a story. But on one occasion his reply was immediate and absolute. He didn't hesitate or equivocate. Matthew recorded this conversation: "[A Pharisee], an expert in the law, asked him a question to test him. 'Teacher, which commandment in the law is the greatest?' He said to him, 'You shall love the Lord your God with all your heart and with all your soul and with all your mind.' This is the greatest and first commandment. And a second is like it: 'You shall love your neighbor as yourself.' On these two commandments hang all the Law and the Prophets" (Matt 22:36–40).

Love God! Love people! This is the gospel in a nutshell! This is the wisdom of the world in four words.

Why don't we emphasize this more in our churches and commentaries and sermons? In these few sentences Jesus summed up all ethical behavior. He gave the solution to all moral problems. He said this is priority number one.

Every decision must be evaluated by the following criteria: If something is loving, it must be said. If something is loving, it must be done.

Even more importantly, if something is not loving, it must not be said. If something is not loving, it must not be done.

This principle trumps all the other requirements and restrictions and legalities of our religious system.

This standard applies in the social realm. It applies in the political realm. It applies in the economic realm. That's why Jesus could "break the Sabbath law" if a person or an animal was suffering on the sacred day. That's why he often socialized and ate with sinners. That's why he always accepted and forgave criminals. That's why he didn't condemn the woman with five husbands and a live-in. That's why he subordinated all the many laws and regulations of the Old Testament to the new law of grace.

36: Handling Anger

Everyone gets angry, but let's consider three productive ways to handle anger.

1. *Use anger rarely.* The scripture says, "One who is quick-tempered acts foolishly" (Prov 14:17).

"One who is slow to anger is better than the mighty, and one whose temper is controlled than one who captures a city" (Prov 16:32).

"Whoever is slow to anger has great understanding, but one who has a hasty temper exalts folly" (Prov 14:29).

Let's not take offense at every little slight or slur. Anger is normal and can even be beneficial, though not if expressed too often.

Our ability to get along with people is a mark of maturity. A radio speaker said, "I often get critical letters or bitter responses, but I realize these people are not really mad at me. Instead, they're mad at someone who hurt them deeply and I just happened to say something that reminded them of that hurt."

It's hard for us to accept the fact that "there but for the grace of God go I." It's hard for us to imagine that we could have been part of the fanatical Nazi Party who executed Jews or that we could be that sick and frightened sociopath who tortured people. We want to divide the world into the good and the bad and place ourselves on the good side. Instead, we must be tolerant of others and use anger rarely.

2. *Use anger appropriately.* Paul says, "Put away from you all bitterness and wrath and anger and wrangling and slander, together with all malice" (Eph 4:31).

Let's always give people the benefit of the doubt. Let's avoid overreaction. One busy woman handled it this way: She and another lady bumped into each other on the street and spilled some packages. She quickly said, "If this was my fault, I'm very sorry, and if it was your fault, that's okay. It's not important enough to bother about."

Most conflicts and irritations are like that. If we have trouble with our car, we don't give up driving. If we have a roof that leaks, we don't abandon the house. Unfortunately, when a couple of people have a disagreement, they are seldom mature enough to let it go or try to work things out.

We must even be careful with apologies. They can be self-righteous and vindictive. Saying "I'm sorry I was angry when you mistreated me" or "I forgive you for the terrible things you did to me" is not an apology. Reserve hostility for truly important matters, and use anger appropriately.

3. *Use anger briefly.* Paul said, "Be angry but do not sin; do not let the sun go down on your anger" (Eph 4:26).

Anger should be short-lived. Don't hold grudges. Bitterness and resentment are killers. Even if an action is unfair and meant to harm, we need to realize it's really the other person's problem and let it go. Releasing the animosity quickly reduces the damage of hatred. So be angry rarely. Handle it appropriately, and hold on to it briefly.

37: Handling Difficult People

"Those who need love the most deserve it the least." What does that mean? Well, it means that those aggravating people who are so hard to live with have many unmet needs. They're defensive, hostile, depressed, full of self-pity, and anxious because no one has ever cared about them. It's the hungry baby who cries, and it's the needy adult who complains.

Difficult people feel inadequate because the significant others in their lives have neglected or abused them. Everyone has needs, and the desperate efforts to get those needs met often lead to antisocial behavior. As Christians, we can help fill those needs. These five actions are important:

1. *When you meet defensive and touchy individuals, absolve them.* This means to forgive and forget. Quit trying to make them feel guilty by holding them to their past.

2. *When you meet hostile and antagonistic individuals, accept them.* This means to take them as they are. Quit judging and trying to change them.

3. *When you meet depressed and pessimistic individuals, affirm them.* This means to reassure and encourage them. Quit demeaning their attitudes and criticizing their actions.

4. *When you meet complaining and miserable individuals, appreciate them.* This means to respect and praise them. Quit taking their contributions for granted.

5. *When you meet anxious and unproductive individuals, approve them.* This means to recognize and support them. Quit blaming and censuring their feelings and behavior.

Yes, aggravating people will remain that way until their basic needs are met. So when you meet that old grouch, try to find his need and fill it. When you meet that person who seems to deserve love the least, give it more graciously than ever. That's what God does. Paul said, "God proves his love for us in that while we still were sinners Christ died for us" (Rom 5:8).

38: Happiness

The psalmist said, "This is the day that the LORD has made; let us rejoice and be glad in it" (Ps 118:24).

Instead, most of us say, "No! I'll only be happy when this occurs or that occurs." We believe there's an ideal moment out there somewhere, and if we can just find it, we'll be happy. But that's not how life works.

1. *An authentic personality makes us happy.* After he had become famous, Irving Berlin met a struggling young composer named Gershwin and offered him a job. But then he quickly added, "If you accept this job, you may develop into a second-rate Berlin. But if you insist on being yourself, someday you'll become a first-rate Gershwin."

We should look for the single spark of individuality that makes us different from everyone else and develop that for all it's worth.

2. *A positive attitude makes us happy.* A little boy with a baseball was overheard talking to himself: "I'm the greatest batter in the world," he bragged. Then he tossed the ball into the air, swung at it, and missed.

"Strike one!" he cried.

Again, he announced, "I'm the greatest baseball hitter ever!" He then threw the ball into the air and swung at it and missed.

"Strike two," he announced.

Undaunted, he picked up the ball, examined his bat, and announced once again, "I'm the greatest hitter who ever lived!" He swung the bat hard but missed for the third time.

"Strike three," he cried.

And then he added, "Wow! I'm a great pitcher!"

Now that's a positive mental attitude.

3. *Relationships make us happy.* If a solitary hermit had ten billion dollars and everything he desired, he still wouldn't be happy. He would need people to rejoice with him in his good fortune. Intimacy and social interaction make us happy.

4. *A purposeful life makes us happy.* True happiness is found in normal daily events that give us a sense of accomplishment and meaning. Paul said, "I have learned to be content with whatever I have" (Phil 4:11).

39: Hiding or Healing?

Does a doctor only allow perfectly healthy specimens into his office? Does an ambulance only transport the able-bodied? Does a hospital throw out all the sick people? That's utter nonsense. Such actions would defeat the whole purpose of medical institutions. Yet we do this very thing in religion. We shun the sick and shoot the wounded.

When Jesus confronted the "anti-sinner" crusade of the first century, he reacted sharply: "When the scribes of the Pharisees saw that he was eating with sinners and tax collectors, they said to his disciples, 'Why does he eat with tax collectors and sinners?' When Jesus heard this, he said to them, 'Those who are well have no need of a physician but those who are sick; I have not come to call the righteous but sinners'" (Mark 2:15–17).

1. *Sin is not for condemning.* Jesus said, "God did not send the Son into the world to condemn the world but in order that the world might be saved through him" (John 3:17).

He also used parables to reduce intolerance, saying, "Which one of you, having a hundred sheep and losing one of them, does not leave the ninety-nine in the wilderness and go after the one that is lost until he finds it? And when he has found it, he lays it on his shoulders and rejoices. And when he comes home, he calls together his friends and neighbors, saying to them, 'Rejoice with me, for I have found my lost sheep.' Just so, I tell you, there will be more joy in heaven over one sinner who repents than over ninety-nine righteous persons who need no repentance" (Luke 15:4–7).

Jesus never, by one word or deed, indicated that his church was to be a museum for saints. Instead, he emphasized over and over again that it was to be a hospital for the sick, a therapy center for the crippled, and a sanctuary for the outcast. He said, "Go out at once into the streets and lanes of the town and bring in the poor, the crippled, the blind, and the lame…. Go out into the roads and lanes, and compel people to come in" (Luke 14:21, 23).

Jesus championed the underdog, saying, "Two men went up to the temple to pray, one a Pharisee and the other a tax collector. The Pharisee, standing by himself, was praying thus, 'God, I thank you that I am not like other people: thieves, rogues, adulterers, or even like this tax collector.'... But the tax collector, standing far off, would not even lift up his eyes to heaven but was beating his breast and saying, 'God, be merciful to me, a sinner!' I tell you, this man went down to his home justified rather than the other, for all who exalt themselves will be humbled, but all who humble themselves will be exalted" (Luke 18:10–11, 13–14).

2. *Sin is not for hiding.* John said, "If we confess our sins, he who is faithful and just will forgive us our sins and cleanse us from all unrighteousness" (1 John 1:9)

Jesus identified himself with common men, not priests. He ministered more in the streets than in the temples. He taught more in the homes than in the synagogues. He conversed more with the unorthodox than with the orthodox.

It's significant that the lowest members of society felt free to come to him with their problems. Why on earth, then, do Christians try to deny their shortcomings? Why do religious organizations cover up their weaknesses? Why is the church more interested in hiding its backsliders than in healing them?

Of course, many self-righteous "do-gooders" will point out our hypocrites, castigate our prodigals, and urge us to abandon our fallen. So what? They did the same thing with Jesus.

Some "holier-than-thou" critics will tell us to "clean house" and excommunicate those who stray, but we must not succumb to the pressure. Any congregation that becomes more concerned about its image than about its ministry ceases to be a church.

3. *Sin is for healing.* James said, "Confess your sins to one another and pray for one another, so that you may be healed" (Jas 5:16).

If there's a disreputable sinner anywhere in the community, then the church should be his haven. Jesus didn't kick Peter out for cursing and lying. Jesus didn't have a heresy trial for doubting Thomas. Jesus didn't even "dis-fellowship" Judas.

You see, sin is not for condemning! Sin is not for hiding! Sin is for healing, and healing can only occur in a nonjudgmental, caring atmosphere.

40: The Holy Spirit

The Holy Spirit is a special gift from God. Jesus said, "If you, then, who are evil, know how to give good gifts to your children, how much more will the heavenly Father give the Holy Spirit to those who ask him!" (Luke 11:13). The Holy Spirit is within us as a comforter, instructor, and guide. Jesus said, "I still have many things to say to you, but you cannot bear them now. When the Spirit of truth comes, he will guide you into all the truth" (John 16:12–13).

The scripture says the Holy Spirit is like a dove (see Matt 3:16). This expression attempts to portray a sacred moment of consecration. The scripture says the Holy Spirit resembles a fire (see Acts 2:3). This expression attempts to portray a powerful, life-changing event.

The illustration of inspired Christians speaking in many languages was intended to emphasize that the gospel of Christ is not for an elect few of one group. It's for all people of every race and nation.

So how can we recognize and utilize the wonderful gift of the Holy Spirit? It's obvious we must remove it from the esoteric, theoretical realm and relate it to real life.

1. When you have a gut-level warning that cautions you of danger, that may be the Holy Spirit.

2. When you have an urge to speak a word of encouragement to a needy person, that may be the Holy Spirit.

3. When you see a problem and have a sense of responsibility to solve it, that may be the Holy Spirit.

4. When your conscience enables you to forgive and reconcile with an associate, that may be the Holy Spirit.

5. When you anxiously pray for help and then have feelings of peace and assurance, that may be the Holy Spirit.

6. When you face difficult decisions and then new information or unusual events influence your choice, that may be the Holy Spirit.

In short, the Holy Spirit works through our own natural mental, emotional, and spiritual faculties to connect us to God.

41: How to Be a Light

Everyone who teaches or ministers has certain distinctive hallmarks that delineate their beliefs and behaviors. Interactions with others must include understanding and respect. Paul said, "Love one another with mutual affection; outdo one another in showing honor. Do not lag in zeal; be ardent in spirit; serve the Lord" (Rom 12:10–11).

Jesus said, "Let your light shine before others, so that they may see your good works and give glory to your Father in heaven" (Matt 5:16).

These guidelines are helpful:

1. *Avoid reaction.* We must never let attacks or counterattacks shape our message. All extremes are dangerous. They often come from pendulum swings that push things "as far as they can go." We must also refuse to engage in arguments and debates, because either/or positions are usually invalid.

2. *Avoid intolerance.* Each person has a unique perspective on life, and each person has a right—indeed, an obligation—to share that perspective. Paul and James emphasized completely different doctrines. Why shouldn't we be allowed to express and emphasize the spiritual aspects that are most meaningful to us?

3. *Avoid negativism.* We should spend very little time criticizing and condemning. Instead, we must offer constructive alternatives. Teachings that don't produce positive results and good fruit must be immediately reexamined and modified.

4. *Avoid rigidity.* We must stand ready to adapt, improve, or even discard any belief if the discovery of new facts warrants such a move. We must be especially skeptical of "comforting" doctrines and try to hold them loosely.

5. *Avoid dogmatism.* We must allow others the same rights we claim for ourselves. If I say a Christian prayer in a public school, then I must graciously allow the Muslim to say his prayers in a public school. If I remove books on atheism, then I must expect atheists to remove books on Christianity. Any form of censorship is "rigging the race."

6. *Avoid sensationalism.* We should recognize that any emotional episode creates a "high," which is inevitably followed by a "low." Whether the highs are induced by internal drugs, such as adrenalin, or external drugs, such as heroin, they take a heavy toll on our bodies and minds. There are no harmless highs. Furthermore, motivation by sensationalism is never permanent.

As witnesses our theology must stand on its own merit, not on its popularity. It must attract people by its truth, not by its excitement. It must hold people by its practical benefits, not by its intriguing mysteries.

We must witness by our life as well as our words. We must let our light shine!

42: How to Fight Fair

Disagreements are inevitable, and they can be either constructive or destructive. We can use them to solve problems or to win arguments. Unfortunately, most of us feel like Lucy when she said, "Well, if I can't be right, then I'll be wrong at the top of my lungs." Nevertheless, the psalmist advises peace and harmony among Christians: "How very good and pleasant it is when kindred live together in unity" (Ps 133:1)

There are at least five possible ways to handle conflicts:

1. *My way:* "I must win. I'm totally right, and you're totally wrong. My way is not merely the best way; it's the only way. My needs are all that matter. My desires are all that count." This agenda emphasizes power, aggression, and selfishness. It can lead to violence, and it never settles anything.

2. *Your way:* "I let you win because I'm insecure, helpless, and afraid. I'll ignore my own needs and pretend to submit. Nevertheless, I will seethe inside and probably find devious methods of retaliation." This agenda emphasizes fear, inequality, and dishonesty. It only leads to bitterness, and it never settles anything.

3. *No way:* "We hide our feelings and deny our differences. We cover up our hurts and promise to 'face that tomorrow.' We withdraw from confrontation and let resentments build." This agenda emphasizes avoidance, procrastination, and delusion. It can lead to lives of quiet desperation, and it never settles anything.

4. *Halfway:* "I win some and lose some. You win some and lose some. I gain a point and concede a point; you gain a point and concede a point. Putting these 'bargaining chips' together, we may be able to create a temporary truce, but we won't secure a permanent peace. I'll still think 'my truth' is better than 'your truth.'" This agenda emphasizes strategies, negotiation, and compromise. It can lead to manipulation, and it seldom settles anything.

5. *Our way:* "We're both concerned about our relationship. We're both in touch with reality. We're both committed to resolving the conflict in

a manner that preserves each person's dignity. We're both determined to reach goals that are mutually satisfying. I don't win; you don't win. We both win! I don't lose; you don't lose. Nobody loses! I don't get my way; you don't get your way. We get 'our way'!"

Paul said, "Finally, brothers and sisters…be restored; listen to my appeal, agree with one another; live in peace; and the God of love and peace will be with you" (2 Cor 13:11). This agenda emphasizes integrity, realism, and accomplishment. It satisfies basic needs and increases intimacy and respect. It settles things!

43: How to Slay Giants

When facing a challenge, we can evade; we can give up; or, like David, we can face it head on. In making this decision the pessimist sees the disadvantages, and the optimist sees the advantages. When Goliath came against the Israelites, the soldiers all thought, "He's so big that we can't kill him." But David looked at the giant and thought, "He's so big that I can't miss him!"

1. *David was confident.* David didn't say, "Someone should do something." He said, "I can do something." Solomon said, "Whatever your hand finds to do, do with your might" (Eccl 9:10).

2. *David was capable.* He had prepared for this moment all his life. He used his past experiences.

> But David said to Saul, "Your servant used to keep sheep for his father, and whenever a lion or a bear came and took a lamb from the flock, I went after it and struck it down, rescuing the lamb from its mouth, and if it turned against me, I would catch it by the jaw, strike it down, and kill it. Your servant has killed both lions and bears, and this uncircumcised Philistine shall be like one of them, since he has defied the armies of the living God." (1 Sam 17:34–36)

You see, his successes with smaller problems had honed his skills and given him expertise to face this large problem.

3. *David was committed.* His faith was strong. He said, "The LORD, who saved me from the paw of the lion and from the paw of the bear, will save me from the hand of this Philistine" (1 Sam 17:37).

We need confidence. We need capability. We need commitment.

The next time you get an egg from the refrigerator, ask yourself this question: "Can an egg fly?" That sounds silly! Everybody knows an egg can't fly! But wait a minute. An egg does indeed have the potential to fly. When new life breaks out of its shell and the wings spread, former eggs do fly every day. In fact, they can soar like eagles.

With confidence, capability, and commitment, this can happen to us.

44: How to Spell *Faith*

Jim loved football. He read about famous football stars. He watched videos. He attended every local game. He visualized himself receiving the Heisman trophy. He believed in his ultimate success. At tryouts, he scrambled for the ball, but to no avail. Three times the runner easily avoided Jim's attempts to bring him down. Jim knew the game, but he had trouble on the field.

Faith and works are not opposites. They are not contradictory. Instead, they're complementary. Faith is the mental part of the equation. Work is the physical part of the equation.

Once, a poor immigrant's son wrote an essay about his dream of owning a successful cattle ranch when he grew up. When his paper was returned from the teacher, it was marked with a big red "F." The teacher believed his was an unrealistic dream because of his life circumstances, and offered to reconsider the grade if he rewrote the assignment.

The boy thought for a long time. Finally, he turned the original paper back in with no changes, saying, "You can keep the 'F.' I'll keep my dream."

Today, that school paper is framed and hangs over the fireplace in his beautiful ranch home.

Faith involves both dreams and deeds.

Let's analyze F-A-I-T-H.

1. *F stands for facts.* The means and the accomplishments must be possible. John said, "This is the boldness we have in him, that if we ask anything according to his will, he hears us" (1 John 5:14).

According to his will means "in agreement with universal principles." Jesus didn't expect God to change the laws of gravity when Satan dared him to jump off the pinnacle of the temple.

According to his will means "in line with reality." It's not like the prayer a little girl prayed, saying, "Please, God, make Boston the capital of Vermont, 'cause that's what I put on the test." That's not possible because it's not factual. Our belief system can't be based on fiction.

2. *A stands for action.* We must do what we can to achieve it. James said, "What good is it, my brothers and sisters, if someone claims to have faith but does not have works? Surely that faith cannot save, can it?" (Jas 2:14).

The "work" is our part of the covenant.

According to legend, a man saw a shop with a sign that read, "Ask and ye shall receive!" He entered and demanded a loaf of sliced bread.

"You don't understand," the clerk replied. "God provides the resources, not the finished product. He gives wheat seeds, not baked loaves."

Jesus didn't expect God to turn rocks into rolls when he was hungry. Yes, there was manna in the wilderness, but the Israelites had to gather it and prepare it for food. Faith must have feet!

3. *I stands for interest.* We must really desire it. Paul said, "Strive for the greater gifts" (1 Cor 12:31).

Once, a young man seeking spiritual insight traveled to India. The sage took him to the river Ganges. The youth expected a mythical ritual, but instead the wise man held him under the water until he finally struggled to the surface, gasping in desperation. "Now, Son," the sage said, "when you want enlightenment as much as you wanted air, you'll find it."

Faith rewards sincere seekers.

4. *T stands for talent.* We must have the ability to do it. Paul said, "We have gifts that differ according to the grace given to us" (Rom 12:6).

Once, a king asked a subject for a contribution. The man gave the king three pennies. That night, he opened his bag to find three pieces of gold. "Oh my!" he said. "I wish I had given him all of my coins."

God can do great things, but he can only use what we give him. Faith requires us to go with our strengths and use our skills!

5. *H stands for hope.* We must have confidence and the expectation of victory. The scripture says, "Faith is the assurance of things hoped for, the conviction of things not seen" (Heb 11:1).

A child celebrating his birthday was excited that he'd recieved two books, a new shirt, and a camera. His mother reminded him, "Honey, no one has given you a camera."

"Well, not yet," he replied, "but Grandma called and told me she was giving me a camera. So I really do own one." And he kept calmly claiming that camera until it actually came a week later.

45: Is Bigger Always Better?

Is bigger always better? Of course not! Is popularity evidence of truth? Of course not! In fact, it's often the reverse. Jesus himself said, "Woe to you when all speak well of you" (Luke 6:26).

Once, as a result of a certain teaching, "many of [Jesus's] disciples turned back and no longer went about with him" (John 6:66).

There are many reasons why productive groups are often smaller and less popular than sensational groups:

1. *Productive movements aren't as exciting.* They don't emphasize mystery and intrigue.

Which sells faster and attracts more readers: a scientific journal or a tabloid magazine with "aliens" on its cover? The tabloid, of course, but is that a true test of its worth? Is the tabloid actually more important and reliable than the scientific journal? Obviously not!

2. *Productive movements aren't as emotional.* They don't appeal to feelings only. It's much easier to persuade with fear and anger than it is with logic and reason. Setting up a "confrontational" atmosphere creates fanatics. Making everyone who differs from us the "enemy" is a powerful manipulation device. This technique is used to enlist soldiers in war and increase voter participation.

Which has better attendance: an academic lecture on interpersonal relationships or a football game between two bitter rivals? The game, of course, but is that a true test of its worth? Is the game actually more important and beneficial over the long term than the lecture? Obviously not.

3. *Productive movements aren't as simplistic.* Their agendas don't lend themselves to slogans. Their issues aren't as black and white. People are more comfortable with a defined purpose that can be easily grasped and repeated. Working to win a hot election is satisfying because the results are immediate and tangible. Working to increase the educational level of society is not as satisfying because the results are not as immediate or tangible.

Which is easier: to chant "Kill the enemy!" or say "Let's try to develop a deeper understanding of our basic differences"? Kill is much easier to chant, of course, but is that a true test of its worth? Is killing actually more constructive than developing deeper understandings? Obviously not!

4. *Productive movements aren't as personally oriented.* They don't depend upon charismatic leaders and sentimental rituals. It's much harder to maintain devotion to abstract principles like justice and truth than it is to a strong charismatic personality. Also, tokens and symbols are essential crutches to most people. These may include placards, crosses, or political buttons.

Which is more likely to inspire loyalty: a flag or a rational principle? The flag, of course, but is that a true test of its worth? Are you actually more likely to solve your problem by waving a piece of cloth than you are by facing reality and making a thoughtful decision? Obviously not!

5. *Productive movements aren't as dogmatic.* Healthy organizations don't demand absolute obedience. They know you can't free people by tying them to some higher authority. They don't require total allegiance, because they know it's only when their members are able to operate efficiently without them that they have succeeded!

Is it easier to train a child to follow your orders instantly and unquestioningly or to help a child become mature enough to make good moral choices on his own without having to rely upon you? The conditioning process is easier, of course, but is that a true test of its worth? Is a child who has been brainwashed to obey actually better off in the real world than a child who has developed the ability to make good decisions on his own? Obviously not!

Sensational tabloids are not better than scientific journals. Emotional football games are not better than educational lectures. Simplistic slogans are not better than profound purposes. Charismatic personalities are not better than moral principles. Dogmatic conditioning is not better than autonomous maturity.

In short, popularity is not a true test of worth! And bigger is not always better! Paul said, "If you think you are standing, watch out that you do not fall" (1 Cor 10:12).

46: Jesus's Ministry Methods

Most of us truly want to share our faith and serve others. Unfortunately, our efforts sometimes seem to do more harm than good. We're like the eager Boy Scout who reported that his good deed for the day was helping a little old lady across the street. "In fact," he added, "I should get double credit because she didn't really want to go."

Instead of providing answers to questions people haven't asked or devising solutions for problems people don't have, let's study Jesus's ministry methods. How did he serve?

1. *Jesus responded to requests.* He didn't go out and collar folks. He didn't rush up to sinners and say, "Hey, man, I'm gonna fix you!"

He knew a person must be ready before help will be accepted. Therefore, he usually let them make the first move. He let them approach him and ask for help.

"Two blind men followed him, crying loudly, 'Have mercy on us, Son of David'" (Matt 9:27).

"A man with a skin disease came to him begging him, and kneeling he said to him, 'If you are willing, you can make me clean'" (Mark 1:40).

A father "begged him to come down and heal his son" (John 4:47).

Even then, he didn't advise or lecture or condemn. He didn't say, "I know just what is wrong with you, and I've got the perfect antidote." Instead, he realized a person needs to discover and express his own problem. He usually asked pointedly, "'What do you want me to do for you?' The blind man said to him, 'My teacher, let me see again'" (Mark 10:51).

2. *Jesus used tools that were available.* Sometimes he accomplished his purpose with a touch. Mark said, "Moved with pity, Jesus stretched out his hand and touched him and said to him, 'I am willing. Be made clean'" (Mark 1:41).

Once, he used a ball of clay: "He spat on the ground and made mud with the saliva and spread the mud on the man's eyes" (John 9:6).

He also used a pool of water when he said, "Go, wash in the pool of Siloam" (John 9:7).

You see, there was no one magic formula, because the cure was not in an object. The cure was in the mind and heart of the sufferer. "Jesus… said, 'Take heart, daughter; your faith has made you well'" (Matt 9:22).

3. *Jesus expected personal responsibility.* Even when a convert wanted to stay dependent, he refused and gave him a new purpose: "The man from whom the demons had gone begged that he might be with him, but Jesus sent him away, saying, 'Return to your home, and declare how much God has done for you'" (Luke 8:38–39).

Jesus knew autonomy, independence, and personal responsibility are important, and his therapy methods reflected this principle.

47: Jesus Respects Diversity

The gospel allows diversity. Diversity includes seeing people as unique individuals, respecting their differences, and evaluating deeper traits.

1. *Jesus saw people as individuals.* He never labeled people by their race, gender, age, or religion. He didn't lump people into stereotypical groups. When he praised the Roman centurion, that didn't mean every Roman military general was faithful. When he admired the Syro-Phoenician woman's response to his inquiry, that didn't mean every person of that nationality was wise. When he appreciated the one grateful Samaritan leper who thanked him, that didn't mean every Samaritan was good-hearted and grateful.

He gave children precedence over priests and scribes. He allowed Mary to discuss theology instead of clean the kitchen. He accepted all kinds of people and knew they were valuable in his ministry. Jesus knew there were worthwhile men and women in every race and culture and religion. He said, "People will come from east and west, from north and south, and take their places at the banquet in the kingdom of God" (Luke 13:29).

He saw individuals, not labels and stereotypes.

2. *Jesus respected differences.* He elevated the status of women, children, and minorities. He complimented the centurion and made Samaritans the heroes of his stories. His disciples ranged from politicians to rebels. These men were so diverse that we wonder how they ever managed to come together in a common cause. Peter and John, for example, could not have been more different. Peter was bold and impulsive, while John was quiet and thoughtful. Most of the disciples were believers, but Thomas seemed to always play the role of a skeptic.

The political differences between Matthew and Simon the Canaanite were potentially explosive. Matthew was a tax collector and a servant of the Roman government, and Simon was a zealot and a rebel. He would have hated Rome and taxes and those who gathered them.

One of the great lessons we learn from Jesus's choice of the Twelve is that God loves all of us.

3. *Jesus evaluated deeper traits.* He looked at the "fruit." He assessed people by their character and productivity, not by their ideology or doctrinal positions. He even declared that the sheep on his right hand were welcome into heaven because their behavior revealed the condition of their hearts: "Then the king will say to those at his right hand, 'Come, you who are blessed by my Father, inherit the kingdom prepared for you from the foundation of the world, for I was hungry and you gave me food, I was thirsty and you gave me something to drink, I was a stranger and you welcomed me, I was naked and you gave me clothing, I was sick and you took care of me, I was in prison and you visited me'" (Matt 25:34–36).

But they were surprised and asked, in essence, "Lord, when did we do any of these things for you?" (see Matt 25:37–39).

Then came the clincher. The king said, "Truly I tell you, just as you did it to one of the least of these brothers and sisters of mine, you did it to me" (Matt 25:40).

Now, this group did not look religious. They didn't act religious. They didn't even know they were religious, but they were, in the best sense of the word. Jesus evaluated deeper traits.

A modern analogy puts it this way: A certain elderly woman went down from Washington to Richmond. She had a flat tire that left her stranded by the side of the road. By chance, a limousine with a bumper sticker that read "Smile, God Loves You" came through. When the occupants saw the stranded woman, they passed by in the far lane without smiling. Likewise, there came a sports car with a bumper sticker saying "Honk If You Love Jesus." That driver passed by without honking.

But a certain Muslim janitor, as he traveled to his job, saw the woman. He had compassion on her, and he stopped his old pickup, which had no bumper stickers, crossed the four-lane highway, and changed her tire.

The woman tried to pay him, but he refused, saying, "If my mom was stranded with a flat tire, I'd want someone to stop and help her out."

Now, which of these three did a "Christian act" for the lady who had a flat tire?

The answer is obvious. The good news of the gospel sees individuals, respects differences, and evaluates deeper traits.

48: The Language of the People

We assume everyone is like us, but they're not. Words and expressions have different meanings in different families and cultures. Paul said, "If in a tongue you utter speech that is not intelligible, how will anyone know what is being said? For you will be speaking into the air" (1 Cor 14:9).

Each person has his own figures of speech and methods of expressing. Some people are more visual; some are more auditory; some are more kinesthetic. People even feel loved in different ways. We must express our affection in ways that make the other person feel accepted and supported.

If we aren't on the same wavelength, people may take things in a wrong way and misunderstand. One woman shared such an experience. She said, "The letter from my British mother-in-law shocked me. I had met her only once and thought she liked me, but evidently I was mistaken. When my husband gave me the letter from his mother, I read it and felt stunned. She had written, 'Paul, it was so nice seeing you and Linda again. She is a very homely girl.' I stopped reading and thought: What a terrible thing to say! I showed the offending sentence to my husband and asked, 'Why did your mother insult me?'

'Mum wasn't insulting you,' he explained. 'That's a compliment.'

'Calling me ugly is a compliment?' I snapped.

He started chuckling. 'Is that what *homely* means here in America? In England it means you are a good homemaker and very hospitable.'

I felt relieved and determined not to be so quick to see slights where none are intended."

Jesus used the language of the people. The scripture says, "With many such parables he spoke the word to them as they were able to hear it; he did not speak to them except in parables" (Mark 4:33–34).

That means he explained his ideas with simple stories. He illustrated his teachings with concrete examples.

Let's use words carefully and express our feelings clearly. Language is important!

49: Leaders or Charlatans?

We must connect ethics with leadership. In both politics and religion, a nice appearance and a glib tongue are not enough. Now, of course, presidents and preachers are fallible human beings. Even so, the scriptures say those in positions of responsibility will be held to higher standards: "From everyone to whom much has been given, much will be required, and from the one to whom much has been entrusted, even more will be demanded" (Luke 12:48).

Since leaders are models and examples, they must be absolutely beyond reproach: "Set the believers an example in speech and conduct, in love, in faith, in purity" (1 Tim 4:12).

In an age of media hype, charisma is king. Nevertheless, the most handsome, charming, persuasive, and exciting person is not necessarily the best leader!

1. *We need leaders with intellectual maturity.* They must have knowledge, understanding, and wisdom. "Can a blind person guide a blind person? Will not both fall into a pit?" (Luke 6:39).

A mature leader emphasizes deep, relevant principles rather than shallow, sensational fads. A mature leader knows that reciting the flag salute doesn't make a person a patriot and singing "Praise Jesus" doesn't make a person a Christian.

2. *We need leaders with emotional maturity.* They must have self-worth and self-confidence. The insecure, power-hungry individual has no place in politics or religion. "Do not lord it over those in your charge, but be examples to the flock" (1 Pet 5:3).

A mature leader can rise above opinion polls and stand utterly alone on unpopular truths if necessary.

3. *We need leaders with social maturity.* They must have a healthy humility that includes tolerance of those who differ and the ability to see all sides of life. "The Lord's servant must not be quarrelsome but kindly to everyone, an apt teacher, patient, correcting opponents with gentleness" (2 Tim 2:24–25).

A mature leader treats people with respect. He never views them as merely contributors, voters, or ego props.

4. *We need leaders with spiritual maturity.* They must have integrity and enormous self-discipline. Honesty and accountability are essential. "Let your priests be clothed with righteousness" (Ps 132:9).

Mature leaders don't desert their posts when the going gets rough. They don't leave churches in debt or turmoil. Jesus says that's how you can distinguish the true leader from the charlatan. The leader stands by through thick and thin, but the charlatan disappears at the first sign of trouble: "The hired hand runs away because a hired hand does not care for the sheep" (John 10:13).

Yes, we do have a crisis in leadership today. It's turning off the electorate, and it's undermining the credibility of the gospel. Unfortunately, we as followers are partially to blame. It's time we said, "Enough is enough! We're not going to take it anymore!" Let's demand honorable leadership! Let's evaluate our elected officials and our pastors and evangelists. Let's quit falling for a smooth line and a pretty face. Let's make our leaders earn our respect!

It's up to each of us to do this, because, as citizens and church members, we get just about what we deserve!

50: Learning from the Animals

In handling social conflicts, we can learn a lot from our furry friends. Let's consider what conditions produce animal attacks? What circumstances cause animals to become dangerous?

1. An animal will attack if it's hungry or thirsty. In other words, when an animal's basic needs are not being met, it becomes dangerous. The same thing is true with human beings. For instance, if you encounter a starving dog, you don't hit it or yell at it. Instead, you throw it some food, realizing that when its needs are met, its animosity will cease.

Likewise, if you encounter a love-starved, approval-hungry person, attacking merely adds to the crisis and does nothing to fill the needs. Instead, discover what is lacking, and try to provide "emotional food."

2. An animal will attack if it's afraid or cornered. When an animal feels that its life or possessions are being threatened, it reacts defensively. If you discovered a wolf nursing her cubs, you wouldn't enter the den. Instead, you'd move away, realizing that when the confrontation is avoided, the animosity will cease.

Likewise, if you discover an insecure, fearful person, don't insist upon a confrontation. Counterattacks only add to the anxiety level and exacerbate the problem. Instead, back off. Give them some space. Defuse the situation by giving the cornered person a way to save face.

3. An animal will attack if it's injured or sick. When an animal is suffering from past hurts or a painful illness, it becomes dangerous. If you found a wounded bobcat, you wouldn't expect it to respond in a pleasant, reasonable manner. Instead, you'd anticipate irrational, hostile behavior. You'd be cautious in your approach, realizing that when healing occurs, the animosity will cease.

Likewise, if you find yourself interacting with a person who has been a victim of abuse or exhibits evidence of a painful neurosis, don't argue or strike back. These tactics are totally useless, since the ill one is not capable of logical mental processes. Pain perverts a person's outlook on reality.

Instead, try to understand and remove the causes of the hurts and set up conditions to promote healing. In short, the solutions to hostile social conflicts lie in mature perceptions and intelligent responses.

Remember, there are always reasons for irrational words and deeds. Most attacks, from both animals and humans, result from the principle of self-protection. Therefore, to resolve destructive conflicts, we must fill basic needs so the person's deprivation doesn't cause internal dissonance, be tolerant and nonjudgmental so the person doesn't feel threatened, and understand and sympathize with the person's previous tragic experiences or health condition so healing can occur.

Unfortunately, the reasons behind attacks may not be as obvious in human beings as they are in animals. People learn to deny their hungers, cover up their fears, and hide their hurts. Since we don't want to admit we are yearning for affection, we act angry. Since we don't want to admit we are scared, we act angry. Since we don't want to admit we're living with pain, we act angry.

Mature individuals must learn to read between the psychological lines and realize that destructive reactions can actually be desperate cries for help.

So when faced with a hostile situation, ask yourself: Is this person hungry for love? Does this person feel threatened? Has this person been hurt? That's the only way the vicious circle can be interrupted.

Even so, some conflicts can't be resolved. You can't fill needs if the person involved won't let you. You can't provide protection if the person involved refuses. You can't offer healing if the person involved rejects it.

Sometimes in the final, sad scenario, you must simply walk away. Jesus said, "If anyone will not welcome you or listen to your words, shake off the dust from your feet when you leave that house or town" (Matt 10:14).

51: Lessons of Life

Most of us remember certain men and women who influenced us in education, but the greatest teacher you'll ever have is life itself. Even though we don't enjoy many of its lessons, all of them can lead to wisdom. Paul realized this when he said, "We know that all things work together for good for those who love God" (Rom 8:28).

Let's consider how ten bad things can teach ten good lessons:

1. *Loneliness:* Think of it as personal free time and use it creatively.

2. *Depression:* Avoid self-pity and learn compassion for others in misery.

3. *Pain:* Accept your vulnerability and feel empathy with hurting humanity.

4. *Sin:* Develop humility and abolish self-righteousness and judgmental attitudes.

5. *Guilt:* Let your regret lead to redress and improvement in the future.

6. *Failure:* Acknowledge your own responsibility and correct your mistakes.

7. *Loss:* Increase your appreciation for what you do have.

8. *Conflict:* Analyze your irritations in order to identify your touchy areas.

9. *Enemies:* Recognize their ruthlessness or pettiness so you can avoid becoming like them.

10. *Doubt:* Admit the difficulty of maintaining a true faith.

We must quit running away from our "teachers." When problems arise, don't deny, don't blame, and don't give up. Instead, learn the valuable lessons they have to teach. The psalmist said, "Before I was humbled I went astray, but now I keep your word.... It is good for me that I was humbled, so that I might learn your statutes" (Ps 119:67, 71).

52: Letters from God

Paul sent a strange message to the church at Corinth. In it he described members of his congregation as "letters from God."

In this interesting analogy he said, "You yourselves are our letter, written on our hearts, known and read by all, and you show that you are a letter of Christ…written not with ink but with the Spirit of the living God, not on tablets of stone but on tablets that are human hearts" (2 Cor 3:2–3).

Few people today read the Bible. Even fewer memorize scriptures and apply them in their lives. Instead, we as Christians are really the only message a lost world reads.

If this is true, then we have an enormous responsibility.

Two young Muslim students came to the United States. A man asked them, "What do you think of America?"

One answered, "I read about all the wealth of America, but I did not believe. I landed in New York; now I believe."

The other young man took up the answer. "I read about the beauty of America," he said, "but I did not believe. I traveled to the Rocky Mountains; now I believe."

"What about Christianity?" the man asked.

The two young men looked puzzled. Then one said, "We read about Christianity too. But we have been here a month, and we still do not believe."

Unfortunately, this is often true, and we are responsible. We are ambassadors from God. Paul said, "We are ambassadors for Christ, since God is making his appeal through us" (2 Cor 5:20)

If each of us is a letter from God to our friends and acquaintances, then what do our lives say?

God wants us to influence the world. Jesus said, "You will be my witnesses…to the ends of the earth" (Acts 1:8).

Fortunately, our ministry efforts multiply. Andrew brought his brother, Simon Peter, to the Lord, and then Simon Peter led three thousand people to the Lord on one day.

So let's be letters from God to our family, to our acquaintances, and to the entire world.

53: Leveling and Listening

Misunderstandings! Is there no end to this vexing problem? Families, churches, businesses, organizations, and nations stay embroiled in useless conflicts because of misunderstandings.

Time is lost because of misunderstandings. People are hurt because of misunderstandings. Energy is wasted because of misunderstandings. For good communication to take place, speakers must level and hearers must listen.

Several things hinder the leveling process:

1. We don't say what we really mean. We beat around the bush and blur the issues. Instead, we need to express our own personal feelings in concise, non-blaming statements.

2. We don't clarify. We expect people to read our minds. They can't! We think others have the same background knowledge and experiences we have. They don't! Instead, we must define our message carefully and completely.

3. We don't illustrate. A complicated, abstract explanation is lost on most listeners. Instead, we need to make it simple and concrete with specific examples.

4. We don't repeat. Advertisers never run their commercials once and then say, "Now, they've heard it! That's enough!" Instead, they run them over and over again. We need to say it many times in many ways.

5. We don't encourage feedback. Communication is a two-way process. We can't evaluate our efforts until we actually hear our message being echoed back to us in the conversation of others.

Then several things hinder the listening process:

1. We don't pay attention. We get distracted. We let our minds wander. We plan our replies. Instead, we need to concentrate on the speaker's verbal and body language.

2. We only get part of the message. We tend to hear what we expect to hear or what we want to hear rather than what is really being said. This is unfortunate because half-truths can be worse than lies.

3. We take it wrong. We let our own prejudices and hang-ups interfere. Words and phrases have many different meanings. If we select the wrong meanings, then we get the wrong message.

4. We twist the facts. We may pick and choose and rearrange the information. Nonsense and falsehoods can be created from the best of material if things are taken out of context.

5. We fail to ask questions. Sometimes we'd rather remain ignorant or misinformed than to admit our confusion. Instead, we should realize that a request for further enlightenment is a mark of intelligence.

One misunderstood word, one misunderstood inflection, one misunderstood gesture and the whole message is distorted.

Misunderstandings destroy good relationships! They sabotage successful endeavors! They exacerbate political unrest! They jeopardize world peace! Life is too short; needs are too great; people are too valuable to let this situation continue. Misunderstandings must be abolished!

"Let the words of my mouth and the meditation of my heart be acceptable to you, O LORD" (Ps 19:14).

54: Little Things Mean a Lot

We may think small things are useless, but that's not true. Little things mean a lot! Moses didn't have an army of tanks and a squadron of fighter planes to defeat the Egyptian pharaoh and free the Israelites. He only had a common shepherd's staff. But he used it.

When God called him, Moses hesitated. Then God asked an important question: "What is that in your hand?" (Exod 4:2).

You see, Moses had something he could use, but he wasn't aware of it. When he was finally willing to use what he had, he became one of the greatest religious leaders of all times.

David didn't have an atomic bomb or an assault rifle to slay Goliath. He just had five little pebbles and a sling, but he used them!

It's interesting to note that David didn't try to fight the giant with the king's weapons or with the soldiers' weapons. Instead, he used the small resources he had, but it was enough to accomplish a great victory.

The little boy who shared his lunch didn't have a gourmet meal of caviar and filet mignon. He only had five rolls and two small fish. But he used them.

Now, in a crowd of all those people, surely many older and wealthier individuals had money and food supplies, but they didn't offer them to Jesus. Only one little boy gave what he had, and the Lord used it.

You may think you have very few talents and skills, but that's not true. The scripture assures us that every person has abilities and gifts. Peter said, "Serve one another with whatever gift each of you has received" (1 Pet 4:10).

Someone said, "Little is much if God is in it!" So what is in your hand? What abilities do you have? What talents do you have? What skills do you have? What knowledge do you have? What experiences have you had that enable you to serve God and others?

It's not necessary to have great things. You don't have to be a best-selling author or a Broadway star or an Olympic athlete in order to serve.

Jesus said the widow who shared only two cents did more than the man with millions who kept it for himself.

55: Logic

There aren't many sermons on logic. In fact, there aren't even many conversations about logic. Logic means the science of correct thought. What could be more important than that? Isaiah said, "'Come now, let us argue it out,' says the LORD" (Isa 1:18).

Some Christians are surprised to discover that Jesus advocated the use of logic. One day, he asked his audience,

> For which of you, intending to build a tower, does not first sit down and estimate the cost, to see whether he has enough to complete it? Otherwise, when he has laid a foundation and is not able to finish, all who see it will begin to ridicule him, saying, "This fellow began to build and was not able to finish." Or what king, going out to wage war against another king, will not sit down first and consider whether he is able with ten thousand to oppose the one who comes against him with twenty thousand? If he cannot, then while the other is still far away, he sends a delegation and asks for the terms of peace. (Luke 14:28–32)

1. *Logic requires thoughtful planning.* This includes linking causes to consequences and preparing for problems. We must not fall for hasty generalizations. For example, one cold day doesn't disprove overall global warming.

We must not accept slippery slope arguments. For example, taking one step onto a roof doesn't necessarily mean you're going to slide all the way to the ground.

We must not let opponents distract us from crucial issues by creating and pointing out fictitious problems.

2. *Logic avoids wishful thinking.* Distorted perception nullifies logic. We correlate events that have no logical connection. This leads to superstition. We believe in luck and chance. We rationalize to reach the conclusion we want to reach. We twist information. We forget certain facts. We make assumptions and come to illogical conclusions.

3. *Logic majors on majors instead of on minors.* Illogical thinkers often emphasize a detail and overlook the core concept. When Orville and Wilbur Wright made history by keeping their invention in the air, they telegraphed their sister in Ohio: "First sustained flight today for fifty-nine seconds." The message continued, "Hope to be home by Christmas."

Their sister hurried to the local newspaper with the great news and gave the editor the telegram. Sure enough, the next day, an article about the Wrights appeared in the paper. The headline read: "Local Bicycle Merchants to Be Home for the Holidays."

The editor had totally missed the point. He overlooked one of the most important moments in aviation history and zeroed in on a trivial detail.

Impulsive decisions, wishful thinking, and majoring on minors lead to falsehood, not truth. Jesus said, "You will know the truth, and the truth will make you free" (John 8:32).

56: Looking for What's Wrong

If you put one dot on a solid white wall and ask people what they see, they'll invariably mention the dot. We tend to see what's "wrong"!

Insecure people turn neutral statements into insults and normal interactions into attacks. They see slurs and put-downs when none exist. This behavior is more common from those with trauma or abuse in the past because that makes the brain's "alarm system" overly sensitive. But Paul said, "If it is possible, so far as it depends on you, live peaceably with all" (Rom 12:18).

The fight/flight response is an innate protective device. When danger is perceived, our body prepares us for defense. This was absolutely necessary for the survival of primitive man. Today, however, it's often counterproductive. Instinctively focusing on what's wrong helped people find and avoid sabertoothed tigers, but today this constant searching for what's wrong sets up a negative lifestyle. There are several reasons for this:

1. *Most childhood conditioning is negative.* Parents and teachers train children by telling them what not to do. What they do right is expected as normal and ignored, while any deviation is punished.

2. *Most of the media focuses on bad news.* Most group conversations consist of complaining and "awfulizing." Paul gave different advice. He said, "Whatever is true, whatever is honorable, whatever is just, whatever is pure, whatever is pleasing, whatever is commendable, if there is any excellence and if there is anything worthy of praise, think about these things" (Phil 4:8).

3. *Most of us judge too quickly.* One man said, "When I was worshiping in an unfamiliar church, a woman near me whispered continually to an older woman beside her. I became annoyed. Later, I heard the preacher greet the younger lady. He said, "How nice to have your mother with us from Lebanon! I'm glad you translated for her during the service."

"I was ashamed of my negative attitude," the critic concluded. Ignorance can cause misinterpretation. "To know all is to forgive all." Let's give everyone the benefit of the doubt. Let's not look for what's wrong!

57: Love Your Enemies!

If there ever was a commandment that seems to be impossible to keep, it's this one: "Love your enemies."

If love can be commanded, then it's obviously not a feeling. The Lord doesn't expect us to feel a certain way toward those who hurt us or insult us. He explains this clearly, saying, "Love your enemies; do good to those who hate you; bless those who curse you; pray for those who mistreat you" (Luke 6:27–28).

In this verse he doesn't tell us we must like them, admire them, enjoy their company, or even have affection for them. In fact, Jesus himself didn't feel any of these things toward those who criticized and harassed him. Instead, he said, "Woe to you, scribes and Pharisees, hypocrites!... You snakes, you brood of vipers! How can you escape the judgment of hell?" (Matt 23:23, 33).

Yet Jesus did love these "enemies." He describes how to demonstrate this kind of love by listing three specific actions:

1. "Do good to them who hate you": This rules out vengeance and retaliation and tells us we must give them food and water if necessary.

2. "Bless them who curse you": This includes being careful to use language that is civil and positive and to always show good will toward those who hurt us.

3. "Pray for them who abuse you": This may be hard to do, but it's important because praying for our enemies can change our own attitude.

The commandment "love your enemies" can be kept because the love Jesus describes doesn't involve our feelings; rather, it requires us simply to treat others with respect.

58: The Lure of Certainty

Most of us have an innate obsession for certainty. We don't like indecisive leaders. We don't like vague answers. We don't like tentative solutions.

Uncertainty produces anxiety; anxiety produces stress; stress makes us miserable. The drive for completion is strong in the human organism. We're frantic to get things nailed down. We're frantic to get things tied up. We're frantic to get things settled.

This lure of certainty pushes us to achieve goals. Unfortunately, it also makes us willing to accept despotic dictators. It makes us willing to accept fallacious answers. It makes us willing to accept quick fixes.

Most of us have three basis needs:

The Need for an Authority Figure

Babies must have caretakers, and many of us never outgrow this dependence. The parent symbol, the father motif, the priest, and the king all promise relief from uncertainty and escape from responsibility. Ideally, the authority figure feeds us, clothes us, and protects us.

Actually, it's a two-edged sword. The authority figure also thinks for us, manipulates us, and ultimately owns us.

Eventually, we must ask ourselves one question: "Am I willing to forego the security of an authority figure in order to experience freedom?"

Scripture promises liberty to Christians: "For freedom Christ has set us free. Stand firm, therefore, and do not submit again to a yoke of slavery" (Gal 5:1).

The Need for Absolute Answers

The simplistic "yes" or "no" response and the positive good or bad evaluation gives us great comfort. It stills our turmoil, absolves our guilt, and makes analysis, reason, and hard choices unnecessary.

But most things aren't absolutely white or black. We must learn to deal with the gray areas. Most things aren't perfectly wonderful or completely terrible. We must discern between "better" and "best" and "worse" and "worst." We must use trial and error and endure the misery of failure.

Eventually, we must ask ourselves one question: "Am I willing to forego the satisfaction of absolute answers in order to find truth?"

Truth is the greatest liberator: "You will know the truth, and the truth will make you free" (John 8:32).

The Need for Perfect Solutions

We reach for the instant remedy, the miracle cure. In fact, accepting a quick fix may resolve our conflicts momentarily, but it will create long-term damage. It's like grabbing a candy bar when you're hungry. This assuages the hunger momentarily, but since it dulls your appetite, you may neglect essential nutrients.

Panaceas don't exist. We must accept gradual improvements and slow, step-by-step progress in lieu of immediate utopias.

Eventually, we must ask ourselves one question: "Am I willing to forego the pleasure of immediate solutions in order to achieve real, permanent success?"

That's what the gospel offers to us: "Whatever is born of God conquers the world. And this is the victory that conquers the world, our faith" (1 John 5:4).

The lure of certainty is a seductive siren. Don't be enticed.

59: Masks, Armors, and Spears

Secret club members wear hoods. Bank robbers wear masks. Trick-or-treaters wear false faces. Why do people wear such disguises? To hide their identity.

Knights of the Middle Ages wore armor. Football players wear helmets. Firemen wear asbestos suits. Why do people wear such coverings? To keep from being hurt.

Ancient warriors carried spears. Soldiers carry guns. Policemen carry tasers. Why do these people carry such weapons? To retaliate if they are threatened.

What do we wear to hide our identity? What masks do we wear? Sometimes we paste on a smiley face to deny our inner pain. We may bully others when we feel insecure. We may rage when we really want to cry. In short, we wear masks to disguise our real feelings.

What do we use to avoid being hurt? What coverings do we use? We display educational awards to make people think we're wise. We use money to buy the respect we haven't earned. We practice workaholism to achieve the self-worth we lack. In short, we wear coverings to hide our fears.

What do we carry to retaliate with when we are threatened? What weapons do we carry? We carry around a hostile attitude to avoid intimacy. We carry a vocabulary full of criticism to put down our associates. We carry a chip on our shoulders to make our friends feel guilty. In short, we carry weapons to intimidate others.

Counterfeit traits permeate our existence. We use pride, rationalization, and excuses to convince ourselves we're okay. We use boastfulness, evasions, and blame to convince others we're okay. We use piety, prayers, and worship rituals to convince God we're okay.

All these masks and coverings and weapons are unnecessary and destructive. As sons and daughters of God, we have unlimited spiritual gifts at our disposal. Paul said, "Be strong in the Lord.... Put on the whole armor of God" (Eph 6:10–11ff.).

You see, when we realize we're created in God's image, we can be ourselves. We can throw away our disguises and coverings and weapons. Then and only then do we have "life." Jesus said, "I came that they may have life and have it abundantly" (John 10:10).

60: Ministering Angels

Angels aren't winged, flying creatures with halos. It's fiction and literature, not Scripture, that give us this idea. In fact, angels aren't even necessarily good beings. The Bible says the devil also has angels. Jesus said, "The eternal fire [was] prepared for the devil and his angels" (Matt 25:41).

The word *angel* is morally neutral. It simply means a messenger or agent. Since God is good, his angels were always sent to bring messages of good news.

An angel gave Hagar good advice: "Return to your mistress" (Gen 16:9).

An angel kept Abraham from making a tragic mistake: "Abraham reached out his hand and took the knife to kill his son. But the angel of the LORD called to him from heaven and said, 'Abraham, Abraham!' And he said, 'Here I am.' He said, 'Do not lay your hand on the boy'" (Gen 22:10–12).

An angel guided Moses: "When we cried to the LORD, he heard our cry and sent an angel and brought us out of Egypt" (Num 20:16).

An angel assured Gideon: "The angel of the LORD appeared to [Gideon] and said to him, 'The LORD is with you'" (Judg 6:12).

An angel provided Elijah with food and water: Elijah "sat down under a solitary broom tree. He asked that he might die, 'It is enough; now, O LORD, take away my life, for I am no better than my ancestors.' Then he lay down under the broom tree and fell asleep. Suddenly an angel touched him and said to him, 'Get up and eat.' He looked, and there at his head was a cake baked on hot stones and a jar of water" (1 Kgs 19:4–6).

Angels comforted and helped Jesus in the wilderness: "Suddenly angels came and waited on him" (Matt 4:11).

In these examples we see that an angel gave good advice to Hagar. An angel kept Abraham from making a tragic mistake. An angel guided Moses. An angel gave assurance to Gideon. An angel provided resources to Elijah. And an angel comforted Jesus.

We can be God's angels. It's our mission to spread the good news of the gospel. It's our mission to encourage and to give assistance. This ministry doesn't require wings or halos!

61: Moral "I" Tests

Defining morality is difficult, but these suggestions may help:

1. *Before engaging in a behavior, determine if it is in harmony with God's Word and God's will.* Ask, "Is this the best or ideal thing for me to do at this time? John said, "Do not imitate what is evil, but imitate what is good" (3 John 11).

2. *Before engaging in a behavior, determine if you will be proud of the action or ashamed of the action.* Ask, "Would I want everybody to know about this?" Paul said, "I do my best always to have a clear conscience toward God and all people" (Acts 24:16).

3. *Before engaging in a behavior, determine if it will make you a better person and the world a better place.* Ask, "Will this really improve my life?" Paul said, "Test everything; hold fast to what is good" (1 Thess 5:21).

4. *Before engaging in a behavior, determine if it could lead to an addiction.* Almost anything can be evil if carried to extremes. Ask, "Am I absolutely sure I can control this if it becomes a habit?" Paul said, "'All things are permitted for me,' but not all things are beneficial. 'All things are permitted for me,' but I will not be dominated by anything" (1 Cor 6:12).

5. *Before engaging in a behavior, determine if what you are doing would harm or help other people.* Ask, "If everyone did this, would the results be positive or negative?" Paul said, "Set the believers an example in speech and conduct, in love, in faith, in purity" (1 Tim 4:12).

If you answered "Yes!" to all five questions, then the behavior is probably moral and appropriate for a Christian.

62: Nobody's Perfect!

You've heard over and over that "nobody's perfect," and it's true. Human beings have weaknesses. Human beings make mistakes. Human beings experience failures.

In fact, the Bible is full of imperfect people. Noah was a drunkard (see Gen 9:20–21). But that wasn't the whole story about Noah: "Noah found favor in the sight of the LORD" (Gen 6:8).

Abraham was a liar (see Gen 12:10–11, 13). Yet "[Abraham]...was called the friend of God" (Jas 2:23).

Jacob was a deceiver (see Gen 27:22–24). Yet he saw "God face to face" (Gen 32:30).

Joseph was an egotist (see Gen 37:5, 9–10). Yet "the LORD was with him...and made [him] prosper" (Gen 39:23).

Moses was a murderer (see Exod 2:12). Yet he chose to dedicate his life to service: "By faith Moses, when he was grown up, refused to be called a son of Pharaoh's daughter, choosing rather to share ill-treatment with the people of God than to enjoy the fleeting pleasures of sin" (Heb 11:24).

David was an adulterer (see 2 Sam 11:2, 4). Yet God said, "I have found David...a man after my heart" (Acts 13:22).

Paul was a persecutor (see Acts 8:3). Yet he was Christianity's greatest missionary.

Peter was a traitor (see Matt 26:69–70). Yet he was a rock in the early church (see Matt 16:18).

You see, since nobody's perfect, we should admit our own imperfections and be tolerant of others' imperfections.

63: No Place to Hide

It has been said that our conscience guides us to avoid bad choices, and reminds us that we might get caught when we behave badly. Well, we do get caught, and our sin does find us out! So what is sin, and what are the consequences of sin?

1. *Sin is anything that harms us.* The writer of Proverbs said, "Whoever finds me finds life…but those who miss me injure themselves" (Prov 8:35–36).

Sin always harms us. Of course, God forgives, but our body, mind, and soul don't, and the consequences remain. So before doing a questionable activity, ask yourself, "Will this strengthen or weaken my body? Will this help or hurt my mental abilities? Will this draw me closer to God or drive me further away from God?"

If you can't give positive, honest replies to these questions, then you should rethink your decision!

2. *Sin is anything that harms others.* Paul said, "It is good not to…do anything that makes your brother or sister stumble" (Rom 14:21).

No one lives completely to himself. Our destructive attitudes and behaviors hurt others. There are no private sins. Before doing a questionable activity, ask yourself, "Will this bring honor or dishonor to my family? Am I willing for my friends to know about this? Will this cause others to be closer to Christ or further away from Christ?"

If you can't give positive, honest replies to these questions, then you should rethink your decision!

3. *Sin is anything that harms God's creation.* Solomon said, "One bungler destroys much good" (Eccl 9:18).

Our destructive attitudes and behaviors hurt the kingdom of God and lower the moral climate of the whole world. Before doing a questionable activity, ask yourself, "Will this bring desirable or undesirable results? Will this help or hinder the kingdom of God? What would happen if everyone did this?"

If you can't give positive, honest replies to these questions, then you should rethink your decision!

64: Of Complaints and Compliments

"You can catch more flies with honey than with vinegar," they say. That's true in the social as well as in the natural world. Compliments encourage and motivate us. Complaints discourage and hamper us. When it comes to relationships, "carrots are much better than sticks."

Paul said, "Encourage one another and build up each other" (1 Thess 5:11). Even so, legitimate complaints can sometimes be necessary. These hints will help make the negative more positive.

1. *A little criticism goes a long way.* Stick to one problem at a time. Don't bring up every shortcoming and mistake from the past. This is devastating and usually causes a person to be become defensive.

2. *Once is enough.* Repeating an accusation over and over again may make you feel better, but it only increases the other person's hostility and frustration. If you say something carefully and clearly, once is enough.

3. *Separate behavior from character.* Never condemn a person's natural or inherent traits. That's both useless and destructive. People can't change their dispositions or their emotions on command. They can only change actions. It's reasonable to say "You must treat that person fairly," but it's not reasonable to say "You must admire that person." It's reasonable to say "Don't shout and hit," but it's not reasonable to say "Don't be angry."

4. *Avoid sarcasm and blame.* Almost any complaint can be expressed respectfully. Making suggestions and asking questions are better than uttering denunciations. Say, "Do you think that was the best response?" or "How could that have been handled differently?"

5. *Earn the right to criticize.* Never criticize unless you know what you're talking about, you are loving and understanding, you are willing to help effect the suggested improvement, and you have already given a lot of support and approval and compliments.

The writer of Hebrews said, "Exhort one another every day…so that none of you may be hardened by the deceitfulness of sin" (Heb 3:13). Yes, compliments are better than complaints. A good rule of thumb is, "Don't offer any criticism that gives you pleasure."

65: Of Sowing and Reaping

Suppose you get a little plastic card in the mail and decide to try it out. You go to the store and see something that catches your eye. You lay down your card, and they hand you a piece of paper. You sign with relief and say, "That wasn't so bad. Why do some people tell me I'll be sorry?" So you continue to use your newly acquired "plastic promise." Then one day, you receive a fat envelope. You open it to find that you're in debt for thousands of dollars. How did that happen? Oh, sure, you charged a few things, but it couldn't have been that much! There must be some mistake.

That's a true picture of reaping what you sow. Paul said, "Do not be deceived; God is not mocked, for you reap whatever you sow" (Gal 6:7). There are three universal principles concerning sowing and reaping:

1. *You reap what you sow.* If you plant cockleburs, you'll reap cockleburs. If you plant daisies, you'll reap daisies. It's as simple as that. You get back what you put in. You can't plant weeds and expect God to turn them into wheat. Sometimes we wish we could reap something different from what we've sown, but that is impossible.

2. *You reap more than you sow.* If you sow a few seeds, you will reap a hundred-fold. One pecan can produce millions of nuts over the years. The multiplying effect is tremendous. There is no such thing as "one small sin." One drink can lead to alcoholism. One wrong choice can lead to drug addiction. One angry word can lead to murder.

Fortunately, it's the same with God. Jesus's ministry was based on this principle. He invested his time and energy in a few ordinary men and women, believing that eventually their lives would influence the world.

3. *You reap later than you sow.* If you plant a garden this morning, you can't begin eating vegetables this afternoon. There's always a delay involved, but sooner or later the effects of your deeds will be felt.

There are no "forgotten sins." Some evils lie dormant for decades before their deadly results become evident. Smoking can cause lung cancer thirty years later. Termites can destroy the foundation of a house before any outward damage is seen. Our influence doesn't die with us! Of both good individuals or evil individuals, it may be said, "He died, but through his faith he still speaks" (Heb 11:4)

66: Our Great Potential

"We're just sinners."

"We can't measure up."

"We're only human."

"We can't be like Jesus."

Such negative statements keep us down. They diminish our potential. Furthermore, they are excuses and copouts. Jesus said, "Be perfect, therefore, as your heavenly Father is perfect" (Matt 5:48).

Now, this doesn't mean we're all to act like sanctimonious, self-righteous saints, but it does mean we're supposed to be growing toward full maturity. The scripture says, "Let us go on toward perfection" (Heb 6:1)

A toddler isn't all he will ever be. He hasn't reached his final height, but he can be just right for this moment if his growth is on track. It's the same with us. If I'm the best I can be at this time, then I'm pleasing to God and at peace with myself. We don't expect a boy to be six feet tall when he's three years old, but we do expect him to be moving in that direction.

Again, it's the same with us. We're to be working on our attitudes and actions. We're to be analyzing our motives and searching our hearts for any hint of pretense or deceit. Paul wasn't perfect, but he was trying. He said, "Not that I have already obtained this or have already reached to goal, but I press on to lay hold of that for which Christ has laid hold of me" (Phil 3:12).

Maturity was his goal for every Christian. He said we are always praying for you "that you may stand mature and fully assured in everything that God wills" (Col 4:12).

Yes, we have great potential. Jesus's prayer for us proves this fact: "The glory that you have given me I have given to them, so that they may be one, as we are one, I in them and you in me, that they may become completely one" (John 17:22–23).

67 Pastor/Laymen Partnerships

Christian congregations and their pastors form a vital partnership dedicated to sharing the gospel. Paul expressed it well when he said, "I planted, Apollos watered, but God gave the growth. So neither the one who plants nor the one who waters is anything, but only God who gives the growth. The one who plants and the one who waters have one purpose, and each will receive wages according to their own labor. For we are God's coworkers" (1 Cor 3:6–9).

Today, the needs are great, and the harvest is ripe. As we cooperate in our ministry, as God's representatives it's important to develop a good working relationship. In order to do this, certain attitudes and skills are required.

1. *We must be understanding.* Solomon had that gift. The scripture says, "I give you a wise and discerning mind" (1 Kgs 3:12).

Everyone has a different viewpoint and perspective on life. We all have different backgrounds and experiences. There are many ways of seeing things and doing things.

Selfishness affects everything we do. It causes bias, prejudice, and selective perception. We take everything personally. We slant facts our way. When I fail, "I'm unlucky." When you fail, "You're lazy." When I succeed, "I'm industrious." When you succeed, "You just got a break."

When selfishness reaches the national level, it becomes discrimination: "Me and my culture are better than you and your culture." "If you're different, then you're wrong." But remember, two things can be different without one of them being wrong. After all, two plus two is four, but one plus three is also four.

Self-worth, self-respect, and self-interest are good and essential traits, but we can overemphasize our own way to the detriment of others, and this leads to conflict.

2. *We must be positive.* Paul said, "May the God of hope fill you with all joy and peace in believing, so that you may abound in hope by the power of the Holy Spirit" (Rom 15:13).

Each person has the opportunity to see a glass as half full or half empty. It's easy to criticize and ridicule, but you can take enough isolated words and deeds from anyone's life to make him look like a scoundrel or a saint. You can take enough statements from any organization's credo to make it look evil or good. You can take enough actions and events from any group's history to make it look destructive or constructive.

3. *We must be focused.* The scripture says, "Poverty and disgrace are for the one who ignores instruction" (Prov 13:18).

Paul felt he had accomplished his goal: "I have fought the good fight; I have finished the race; I have kept the faith" (2 Tim 4:7).

We must not lose sight of our mission. Our combined goal should override minor differences in personalities and beliefs.

68: People Need People

All of us need people. Let's consider five types of relationships in the life of Paul.

Stephen

Stephen was a witness and a great influence on Paul—even while he was still Saul, the unbeliever. That impression was powerful and long-lasting. The scriptures say, "Stephen [was] full of grace and power" (Acts 6:8).

Later, Paul referred to this incident, saying, "While the blood of your witness Stephen was shed, I myself was standing by, approving and keeping the coats of those who killed him" (Acts 22:20).

Stephen was probably unaware that his testimony led to Paul's conversion, but it did. What if Stephen had not been faithful? Everyone needs a dedicated Christian example.

Ananias

An unknown man named Ananias was the first person to accept Paul after his conversion. When Paul had that strange experience on the way to Damascus, he was confused and broken. But Ananias placed his hands on Saul and said, "Brother Saul."

Paul gave him credit for his generous spirit, saying, "Ananias…[was] a devout man according to the law and well spoken of by all the Jews living there" (Acts 22:12).

Ananias saw Paul's potential and was willing to give him a chance. Everyone needs a mentor who believes in them.

Barnabas

Barnabas was a good friend, who helped and encouraged Paul. Even more importantly, he was willing to confront and oppose Paul when he believed he was wrong. Many people were suspicious of Paul when he started preaching. In fact, they tried to kill him. That's when Barnabas came to his aid and formed a partnership. The scriptures say, "[Barnabas] was a good man, full of the Holy Spirit and of faith.… Then Barnabas went to Tarsus to look for Saul, and when he found him he brought him to Antioch. So it was that for an entire year they met with the church and taught a great many people" (Acts 11:24–26).

Everyone needs an honest friend!

Silas

Silas was Paul's associate for many years. He shared in his good times and bad times. The scriptures say, "Paul chose Silas and set out.... He went through Syria and Cilicia, strengthening the churches" (Acts 15:40–41).

Paul and Silas made a great team. They accomplished a lot in their mission endeavors. Everyone needs a dependable associate.

Timothy

Timothy was Paul's protégé. He was the "son" Paul never had. Fortunately, Timothy justified Paul's faith in him. Paul first met Timothy when he was very young. The scriptures say, "There was a disciple named Timothy, the son of Jewish woman who was a believer, but his father was a Greek.... Paul wanted Timothy to accompany him" (Acts 16:1, 3).

Paul was passing the torch to the next generation. Everyone needs a protégé who can carry on after them.

Each of these individuals had a significant influence on Paul's life. What individuals have been significant in your life?

69: The Prodigal Son's Father

In the parable of the prodigal son, we see a father with open hands, open arms, and an open heart.

Open Hands

This dad was wise enough to know that the way to keep his children was to open his hands and let them go. The scripture says, "The younger of them said to his father, 'Father, give me the share of the wealth that will belong to me.' So he divided his assets between them. A few days later the younger son gathered all he had and traveled to a distant region, and there he squandered his wealth in dissolute living" (Luke 15:11–13).

This father did not try to locate his son and drag him home. Instead, he allowed him to determine his own course. The father did not come to his rescue during the financial stress that followed.

The scriptures say, "No one gave him anything.... He came to his senses" (Luke 15:16–17).

We harm our children by preventing them from suffering the consequences of their own mistakes. When a teenager gets a speeding citation, he should pay for it. When he wrecks his car, he should have it fixed. When he gets suspended from school, he should accept his punishment without parental protests to the school.

We learn from adversity. The parent who is too anxious to bail his child out of difficulty is doing him a disservice.

Some parents hold such tight control that they lose their children. This dad was wise enough to let him go.

Open Arms

When the boy came home, the father ran to meet him with open arms. The young man had squandered his inheritance, bringing shame to his father and family.

When he was destitute, he had accepted the lowest possible job for a Jew—feeding swine—in order to stay alive. He had hit rock bottom.

Nevertheless, his father wasn't standing at the gate, glaring down the road and muttering, "You just wait until I get my hands on that kid! He's going to pay for what he's done!"

The scripture says, "So he set off and went to his father. But while he was still far off, his father saw him and was filled with compassion; he ran and put his arms around him and kissed him. Then the son said to him, 'Father, I have sinned against heaven and before you; I am no longer worthy to be called your son.' But the father said to his slaves, 'Quickly, bring out a robe—the best one—and put it on him; put a ring on his finger and sandals on his feet. And get the fatted calf and kill it, and let us eat and celebrate, for this son of mine was dead and is alive again; he was lost and is found!' And they began to celebrate" (Luke 15:20–24).

The father welcomed his son home without belittling him or demanding reparations. Instead, he revealed the depth of his love by saying, "He was lost and is found!"

Open Heart

The most important characteristic of this father was his open heart. During the celebration he was outside assuring the older brother that he was also loved and supported.

We need more fathers with open hands, wise enough to let children go when the time comes.

We need more fathers with open arms, always ready for a new beginning.

We need more fathers with open hearts, providing understanding and encouragement.

Our heavenly Father has open hands toward us. We are free to disobey. He has open arms. He meets us with total forgiveness. He has an open heart. He is a constant presence in our lives.

70: The Pursuit of Happiness

Happiness is not guaranteed. In fact, until about one hundred years ago, it was not even expected! People lived hard, painful lives, toiling from daylight to dark just to survive. Disease and death were the norm, not the exception.

When Jefferson wrote that all men are entitled "to the pursuit of happiness," it was a strange and controversial idea. Today, however, most people think perpetual happiness is their inalienable right. They will not accept frustration, disappointment, or delayed gratification. This can lead to problems.

Researchers have discovered that a "happy outlook" is partly genetic. About fifty percent of our emotions depend upon traits we're born with. The factors that contribute to the other fifty percent include:

1. *Autonomy:* Being able to control at least some aspects of our lives is important. Research shows that even babies who could control what they saw were happier than those who couldn't. A sense of helplessness leads to depression. Jesus said, "If the Son makes you free, you will be free indeed" (John 8:36).

2. *Relationships:* We are made for human connections. People with supportive families and friends rate themselves as much happier than those who are lonely and isolated. The scripture says, "Two are better than one because they have a good reward for their toil. For if they fall, one will lift up the other, but woe to one who is alone and falls and does not have another to help" (Eccl 4:9–10).

3. *Spirituality:* Having faith in something larger than ourselves is also essential to happiness. A commitment that gives purpose in our lives leads to fulfillment. The scripture says, "The joy of the LORD is your strength" (Neh 8:10).

There are several things that do not lead to happiness. Surprisingly, money doesn't necessarily make us happy. Now, extreme poverty is devastating, but after a certain point, where basic needs are met, materialism is a bummer. Many people who have won great riches rated their lives as worse off afterward. Jesus said, "Those who want to save their life will lose it, and those who lose their life for my sake will find it" (Matt 16:25).

Leisure doesn't make us happy! Having some time for relaxation and recreation is good, but too much is a bad thing. Busy people are invariably happier than those who have little to do. James said, "Be doers of the word and not merely hearers who deceive themselves" (Jas 1:22).

Fame certainly doesn't make us happy! Notoriety often backfires after the first excitement wears off. People who achieve a lot of press feel manipulated and used. Soon, they begin to seek anonymity and normality. The scripture says, "Pride goes before destruction and a haughty spirit before a fall" (Prov 16:18).

Happiness seems to be a byproduct, not a goal. Becoming an autonomous being connected to others and having purposeful activities are the best ways to experience happiness.

71: Rageholics

Angry people cause much of the pain and violence in our world. They destroy marriages, commit crimes, and instigate wars. Hostility can have a genetic factor. Some people are chemically predisposed toward greater fight/flight reactions. People are also likely to model volatile parents. Others are more prone to tirades because they have been rewarded for their outbursts.

There are three types of "rageholics":

1. *Some have temper tantrums.* These people act like two-year-olds. They've learned they can get their way by kicking and screaming. This is learned behavior. Without an audience and a response, they soon subside.

2. *Some are control freaks.* These people are the traditional bullies. They are usually insecure. When they sense a threat, they handle their inadequacies by blustering and overreacting. These tyrants can't verbalize specifics, so when confronted, they usually mutter something incoherent and cool off.

3. *A few are time bombs.* These people are the most dangerous. They have a long history of repressed anger. Years of oppression and an accumulation of mistreatment lead to an inevitable explosion.

Anger itself is a legitimate emotion, but when we feel anger, we must decide what to do with it. Should we let it all hang out, or should we keep it all bottled up?

Well, first ask, "Is this anger justified?" If the matter is not really important, then action is not required. In this case, dismiss the anger before it settles into resentment. If there is a legitimate reason for your response, then assert yourself and act in a positive way to correct the unfair situation. If you recognize and use your anger productively, then you won't become a "rageholic." James said, "Let everyone be quick to listen, slow to speak, slow to anger, for human anger does not produce God's righteousness" (Jas 1:19–20).

72. Retaliation or Annihilation

Do we have built-in retaliation urges? Such automatic defense mechanisms were probably essential for survival in a primitive world. Unfortunately, with modern guns and bombs, retaliation can quickly become annihilation. The scripture says, "One given to anger stirs up strife, and the hothead causes much transgression" (Prov 29:22).

This innate "warring instinct" causes us to disagree, argue, and crusade. It emphasizes problems, magnifies differences, and creates conflicts where none exist. We seem to need controversy. From football to chess, we seek competition. From schoolyard skirmishes to political battles, we thrive on confrontation. From showdowns to shootouts, we rush to take sides. What is there about human beings that perpetuates this combativeness?

1. *The risk factor:* Some people have low levels of certain chemical elements. The threats and challenges produce a high that temporarily satisfies this depletion.

2. *The meaning factor:* Everyone needs a purpose, a cause, a reason for being! When we lack our own personal plans and projects, we welcome the opportunity to join a movement with a ready-made agenda.

3. *The decision factor:* We hate to make difficult choices between right and wrong. When a crisis arises, however, there's usually a clear-cut issue at stake. A "Pearl Harbor" event sets up a definite "us versus them" situation. The decisions are already made, and the lines are already drawn. Everyone is aligned as "for and against." There are no confusing "gray areas" or uncertainties to deal with. We know where we stand, and that's satisfying.

4. *The safety factor:* When we identify ourselves with one of the "sides," we immediately have a large support group of like minds. This is comforting.

So are we going to live for temporary highs? Are we going to get our meaning from prepared agendas? Are we going to let others make decisions for us? There are alternatives. Conflicts and crusades and wars are not inevitable. It's possible to live without confrontation. We must curb our combativeness. If we don't, our retaliation may become annihilation. Paul said, "If it is possible, so far as it depends on you, live peaceably with all" (Rom 12:18).

73: Seven Fundamentals of Faith

We hear so much about the "fundamentals of faith," but too often these fundamentals are so trivial and detached from real life that Christianity is losing its credibility. These are a few valid fundamentals:

1. *Respect and love:* In a world with so much contempt and hatred, we need a faith that emphasizes respect and love for individuals. The scripture says, "Honor everyone. Love the family of believers" (1 Pet 2:17).

2. *Justice and compassion:* In a world with so much injustice and unconcern, we need a faith that emphasizes justice and compassion. The scripture says, "Render true judgments, show kindness and mercy to one another" (Zech 7:9).

3. *Responsibility and generosity:* In a world with so much selfishness and greed, we need a faith that emphasizes responsibility and generosity. The scripture says, "We must support the weak" (Acts 20:35).

4. *Tolerance and opportunity:* In a world with so much intolerance and discrimination, we need a faith that emphasizes tolerance and opportunity. The scripture says, "God has shown me that I should not call anyone profane or unclean" (Acts 10:28).

5. *Unity and peace:* In a world with so much hostility and conflict, we need a faith that emphasizes unity and peace, "making every effort to maintain the unity of the Spirit in the bond of peace" (Eph 4:3).

6. *Truth and wisdom:* In a world with so much ignorance and propaganda, we need a faith that emphasizes truth and wisdom. The scripture says, "Buy truth, and do not sell it; buy wisdom, instruction, and understanding" (Prov 23:23).

7. *Courage and hope:* In a world with so much apathy and despair, we need a faith that emphasizes courage and hope. The scripture says, "Be strong, and let your heart take courage" (Ps 31:24).

How does your faith measure up? Are these the core values that are taught and practiced in your church? If not, why not?

74: Sharing the Key

The scriptures say a lot about keys. Jesus said, "I will give you the keys of the kingdom of heaven, and whatever you bind on earth will be bound in heaven, and whatever you loose on earth will be loosed in heaven" (Matt 16:19).

He also said, "Woe to you experts in the law! For you have taken away the key of knowledge; you did not enter yourselves, and you hindered those who were entering" (Luke 11:52).

In Revelation, Jesus said, "I am the First and the Last and the Living One. I was dead, and see, I am alive forever and ever, and I have the keys of Death and of Hades" (Rev 1:17–18).

As Christian witnesses, we too hold the key to a storehouse filled with food, medicine, and information. It's hard to watch helplessly as hungry people starve, sick people die, and ignorant people make destructive decisions. It's frustrating to hold the key that can solve serious problems and prevent terrible tragedies, but no one wants to use it.

It's tragic to watch people beat on the lock with a hammer while you say over and over again, "I have the key, mister. Let me open the door," but no one pays attention. We have the resources to fill deep needs, but no one wants them until it's too late. Most people will not act until a crisis arises, but by then their reputations, careers, marriages, and lives are often in shambles.

Most people only beg for help after disaster strikes in the form of divorce, crime, drugs, and delinquency. After the damage is done, you can't expect a quick fix. As the old saying goes, "It's too late to shut the gate after the horse is out of the pasture."

1. *To individuals, Jesus would say:* Do you ever feel guilty? Do you have trouble with anger, depression, or panic attacks? Are you confused at times? Do decisions upset you? Do you want to find your strengths and overcome your weaknesses?

Believe it or not, you can discover the reasons for your hangups and improve your life by following Jesus's example.

2. *To married couples, Jesus would say:* Do you want to have a good relationship? Are you and your mate as different as daylight and dark?

Does communication ever break down? Would you like to settle conflicts more productively? Do you have in-law trouble? Do the two of you ever disagree on financial matters?

These common problems have specific causes that can be solved by following Jesus's admonition about love and respect.

3. *To parents, Jesus would say:* Do you have problems with your children? Do they have temper tantrums? Are they hyperactive? Is there sibling rivalry in your home? What are your worst fears for your children? Is peer pressure a factor?

There are discipline methods that work if you are willing to obey Jesus's principles. Don't wait until it's too late!

Jesus offers you the key to a successful life! Will you accept it?

75: Sins of Omission

Sins of omission are things we have not done that we should have done. These sins are serious. In Jesus's parable, one man hid his talent in a hole in the ground instead of investing it. When the master came back, he said, "You wicked and lazy slave!... You ought to have invested my money with the bankers, and on my return I would have received what was my own with interest. So take the talent from him, and give it to the one with the ten talents" (Matt 25:26–28). Now, this man had done nothing wrong, but he *had* neglected to do something right. His was a sin of omission!

In Jesus's parable of the rich man and Lazarus, "There was a rich man...who feasted sumptuously every day. And at his gate lay a poor man named Lazarus, covered with sores, who longed to satisfy his hunger with what fell from the rich man's table.... The poor man died and was carried away by the angels to be with Abraham. The rich man also died and was buried. In Hades, where he was being tormented, he lifted up his eyes and saw Abraham far away with Lazarus by his side. He called out, 'Father Abraham, have mercy on me, and send Lazarus to dip the tip of his finger in water and cool my tongue, for I am in agony in these flames.' But Abraham said, 'Child, remember that during your lifetime you received your good things and Lazarus in like manner evil things, but now he is comforted here, and you are in agony" (Luke 16:19–25).

Again, the scriptures don't accuse the rich man of committing a sin. Instead, he was accused of neglecting the poor man in need. His was a sin of omission!

In Jesus's parable of the ten virgins, five irresponsible girls took their lamps but did not take any oil with them. The bridegroom was late, and they all fell asleep. When the bridegroom arrived, the virgins who were ready went in with him to the wedding banquet. And the door was shut (see Matt 25:3, 5–12).

Now, those who were shut out had not committed a sin. They didn't steal their oil or lie about their situation. Instead, they had neglected to have proper foresight and make preparation. Theirs was a sin of omission.

For most of us, sins of omission are more prevalent than sins of commission. But, remember, "Anyone, then, who knows the right thing to do and fails to do it commits sin" (Jas 4:17).

76: The Status of Christians

The status of Christians is one of the most misunderstood concepts of religion. Yet it is a crucial and essential teaching of the gospel.

1. *We are not slaves.* We do not have to say, "Yes master. I'll give you my unquestioned obedience." Instead, we are kings and priests. This means we are totally autonomous. We are in control. The scripture says we are "kings and priests unto God" (Rev 1:6 KJV).

2. *We are not immature children.* We are mature sons and daughters of God—absolutely equal to Jesus in every respect. Jesus said, "Whoever does the will of God is my brother and sister and mother" (Mark 3:35).

Paul said, "Those whom he foreknew he also predestined to be conformed to the image of his Son, in order that he might be the firstborn within a large family" (Rom 8:29).

The writer of Hebrews said, "Jesus is not ashamed to call them brothers and sisters" (Heb 2:11).

We have Jesus's ability and power. He said, "The one who believes in me will also do the works that I do and, in fact, will do greater works than these" (John 14:12). We have the same access and relationship to God that Jesus has. He said, "I do not say to you that I will ask the Father on your behalf, for the Father himself loves you" (John 16:26–27).

We also have the responsibility to live and serve as Jesus did. John said, "As he is, so are we in this world" (1 John 4:17).

3. *We are not servants or second-class citizens.* Instead, we are friends, agents, and ambassadors for God, authorized to represent and speak for him. Jesus said, "You are my friends if you do what I command you. I do not call you servants any longer, because the servant does not know what the master is doing, but I have called you friends, because I have made known to you everything that I have heard from my Father" (John 15:14–15). In fact, "God said, 'Let us make humans in our image, according to our likeness.… God created humankind in his image, in the image of God he created them; male and female he created them" (Gen 1:26–27).

Our status is completely opposite to the traditional view that we are wretched, sinful creatures groveling before a vengeful deity.

77: Steps to Failure

A Sunday school teacher asked her children, "Now, boys and girls, what do we have to do before we can be forgiven of our sins?"

"Well," one little boy said, "first you gotta sin."

We all sin, and Peter was no exception. The terrible night began when Judas betrayed Jesus.

Peter tended toward arrogance. He often compared himself to others. He had publicly boasted that even if everyone else deserted, he certainly wouldn't. He said, "Even though I must die with you, I will not deny you" (Mark 14:31).

Now, Peter probably thought he was being honest. At that moment he sincerely believed he would be loyal. It's easy to have confidence before the crisis. Jesus had specifically instructed him to pray for strength, but instead he had slept.

The scripture says, "Peter had followed him at a distance, right into the courtyard of the high priest, and he was sitting with the guards, warming himself at the fire" (Mark 14:54).

When we follow at a distance, it becomes easier and easier to fall away. Many scriptures admonish us to stay close to the Lord: "Let us approach with a true heart in full assurance of faith, with our hearts sprinkled clean from an evil conscience" (Heb 10:22).

When people begin to miss church and neglect Bible reading and prayer, their priorities gradually change, and the world takes over. Those who follow at a distance soon backslide and lose their spiritual influence.

Peter was separated from his support group in the courtyard of the high priest, sitting with the officers and warming himself at the enemies' fire. He succumbed to negative peer pressure. The psalmist said, "Happy are those who do not follow the advice of the wicked or take the path that sinners tread or sit in the seat of scoffers" (Ps 1:1).

The other disciples were scattered. All those around Peter at that time were unbelievers, and we tend to become like the people we are with. Paul said, "Do not be mismatched with unbelievers. For what do righteousness and lawlessness have in common?" (2 Cor 6:14).

If Peter had kept a diary, one dark page might read this way: "I'm a wretched man! How miserably I have failed. Jesus told me I would deny him three times before dawn, but I didn't believe him. I bragged, 'Oh, no! Even if I have to die, I will never disown you.' I really meant it. But when he asked me to watch while he prayed, I went to sleep.

"I'm ashamed. I ran away when men came to arrest him. Why do I always do the wrong thing? I was warming my hands by a fire in the courtyard when I noticed a servant girl staring at me. Suddenly she said, 'Aren't you one of that man's disciples?'

"I was terrified. 'No! I'm not!' I exploded. I went over into a dark corner to avoid further questions. I huddled there, too scared to breathe. But another girl said, 'This fellow is one of them.' Just then, I heard a rooster crow."

Yes, Peter failed, but all of us are at risk of failure. Are you ever overconfident? Do you follow at a distance? Do you associate with the wrong crowd?

These are steps leading to failure. Fortunately, Jesus forgave Peter and enabled him to win thousands of souls and write part of the New Testament.

He can do the same for us!

78: The Strange Gospel of Jesus

Jesus did not bring a typical religious message. He did not give a list of rules and regulations. He did not issue a lot of taboos and threats. He did not criticize or condemn sinners. In fact, Jesus never preached against any of the prevalent evils of the day, such as prostitution, promiscuity, or drunkenness. He knew these were symptoms, not basic problems. He knew most overt sins are attempts to fill legitimate human needs in unhealthy ways. He knew most people already feel guilty and ashamed. So instead of criticism and threats, Jesus brought good news.

The angels at his birth said, "I am bringing you good news of great joy for all the people" (Luke 2:10).

Jesus believed the propagation of this good news was his divine purpose. He said, "I must proclaim the good news of the kingdom of God…for I was sent for this purpose" (Luke 4:43).

So what is this good news? What are the positive, productive Christian doctrines that fill desperate human needs? What does Jesus offer to hurting people?

1. *Total acceptance:* "Anyone who comes to me I will never drive away" (John 6:37).

2. *Unconditional love:* "No one has greater love than this, to lay down one's life for one's friends" (John 15:13).

3. *Infinite value:* "You are of more value than many sparrows" (Matt 10:31).

4. *Absolute security:* "I give them eternal life, and they will never perish. No one will snatch them out of my hand" (John 10:28).

5. *Immediate forgiveness:* "If we confess our sins, he who is faithful and just will forgive us our sins" (1 John 1:9).

6. *Steadfast support:* "I am with you always, to the end of the age" (Matt 28:20).

7. *Reliable guidance:* "The Holy Spirit, whom the Father will send in my name, will teach you everything" (John 14:26).

8. *Specific purposes:* "You will be my witnesses…to the ends of the earth" (Acts 1:8).

9. *Eternal hope:* "All things can be done for the one who believes" (Mark 9:23).

These are the deep psychological assurances that can fulfill us, change us, and empower us. Jesus spent all the years of his life on earth spreading this message.

Furthermore, Jesus told us, as his witnesses and followers, to continue spreading this message: "Go into all the world and proclaim the good news to the whole creation" (Mark 16:15).

79: Sunny Days or Stormy Nights?

Anybody can sing on sunny days, but it's what we do on stormy nights that reveals the depth of our Christian commitment. Jesus knew this was the test and warned us over and over again that life isn't always fair: "Blessed are you when people revile you and persecute you and utter all kinds of evil against you falsely on my account" (Matt 5:11).

In other words, good deeds aren't always appreciated. Honest intentions aren't always enough. The best efforts aren't always rewarded! You'll be misunderstood! You'll be misquoted! You'll be falsely accused! Many who deserve success will receive failure. Many who deserve praise will receive criticism.

Coping with such inequities is hard, but these principles may help:

1. *Depersonalize the issue.* Remember, we are not the nucleus of the universe. Kingdom purposes are more important than our ego! The feelings and hurts and frustrations that are significant to us right now may be inconsequential in the eternal scheme of things!

2. *Keep things in perspective.* This temporary problem may not be as terrible as it looks. Those we consider to be our enemies may not be as evil as they appear. Current events may not be as catastrophic as they seem to be on the surface. Time heals, and things have a way of sorting themselves out. Saner outlooks and more moderate agendas tend to gain control in the long run.

3. *Get up and go on.* Don't dwell on the past and brood over your injuries. Don't check out of productive endeavors simply because you lost a round or experienced rejection. Continue to participate in constructive activities. Your course may change, but life continues, and the future may be better.

Yes, anybody can sing on sunny days, but it's those stormy nights that provide our best opportunity for witness. Paul said, "Set the believers an example in speech and conduct, in love, in faith, in purity" (1 Tim 4:12).

The world is watching!

80: Talk or Walk?

Is your "lip service" different from your "leg service"? There has always been a gap between our "talk" and our "walk." Jesus said, "This people honors me with their lips, but their hearts are far from me" (Matt 15:8).

You see, being a Christian is a serious matter. It's a way of life. Yet many people see absolutely no connection between Sunday's sermon and Monday's actions. Many people would be utterly astonished to find out they are actually expected to live by the beliefs they espouse.

Too many of us love to attend church and hear preachers say, "Jesus can change your life," but then we are hostile toward any person who really does change his life!

Some people yell, "Amen!" when a preacher says you must be "born from above" (John 3:3), but then they are suspicious of any person who truly does attempt to leave his past and start anew.

Some people passionately believe the Bible, which says, "Go, sell your possessions, and give the money to the poor" (Matt 19:21), yet they call any person who does that an "idealistic fool."

A lot of people claim to believe the Bible, which says, "Be steadfast, immovable, always excelling in the work of the Lord" (1 Cor 15:58), yet they call any person who lives that way a "crazy fanatic."

You see, most of us believe that "whoever becomes humble like this child is the greatest in the kingdom of heaven" (Matt 18:4), but we live by "might makes right."

Most of us believe the scripture that says, "Do not resist an evildoer" (Matt 5:39), but we live by "do unto others before they do unto you."

Most of us believe the scripture that says, "Love your enemies and pray for those who persecute you" (Matt 5:44), but we live by "don't get mad; get even."

Most of us believe the scripture that says, "Do not store up for yourselves treasures on earth" (Matt 6:19), but we live by "money is power."

We talk a good religion, but we are scared of seeing it put into practice! If you saw a real Christian—one who was foolish enough to take the gospel seriously—would you praise him or persecute him? Would you compliment him or criticize him? Would you support him or ridicule him?

Are you sure?
81: Three Principles of Behavior

Self-Respect: Each of us develops a self-image, and then we live up to or down to that self-image. If we really believe we're children of God, we'll live up to that status. The scripture says, "God created humankind in his image, in the image of God he created them; male and female he created them" (Gen 1:27). John said, "To all who received him, who believed in his name, he gave power to become children of God" (John 1:12).

"It is that very Spirit bearing witness with our spirit that we are children of God, and if children, then heirs: heirs of God and joint heirs with Christ" (Rom 8:16–17).

Integrity: Those who believe one way and act another way experience a painful condition called "cognitive dissonance." If we are hypocrites, we will live miserable, nonproductive lives. Jesus said, "No one can serve two masters, for a slave will either hate the one and love the other or be devoted to the one and despise the other. You cannot serve God and wealth" (Matt 6:24). Jesus also says, "This people honors me with their lips, but their hearts are far from me" (Matt 15:8).

Paul said, "They profess to know God, but they deny him by their actions" (Titus 1:16).

Forgiveness: If we feel guilty, we project our bad feelings onto others and blame them for the problem. If we feel forgiven, that will make us more tolerant and empathetic. Jesus said, "How can you say to your neighbor, 'Let me take the speck out of your eye,' while the log is in your own eye? You hypocrite, first take the log out of your own eye, and then you will see clearly to take the speck out of your neighbor's eye" (Matt 7:4–5).

Paul says, "You are without excuse, whoever you are, when you judge others, for in passing judgment on another you condemn yourself, because you, the judge, are doing the very same things" (Rom 2:1). He also said, "Bear with one another and, if anyone has a complaint against another, forgive each other; just as the Lord has forgiven you, so you also must forgive" (Col 3:13).

If we have self-respect, if we have integrity, and if we offer forgiveness, we will be mature and productive.

82: Three Useless Expressions

Most of us waste a lot of time and energy making useless statements and asking useless questions.

Sometimes we look back at things we cannot change and say, "If only!" We feel guilt for past mistakes and regret for poor decisions.

Once, two elderly women died. Both had sons. One son grieved and said, "If only I had sent my mom to Florida this winter instead of letting her live here in the cold, she might be alive." The other woman's son said, "If only I had kept my mom home instead of letting her travel to Florida this winter, she might be alive."

We can't put life on instant replay. We can't always know what would have been the better choice. And second-guessing ourselves only makes us miserable.

Sometimes when we are in a crisis, we wring our hands and say, "Why me?" We feel angry that life is unfair and are envious of others around us who seem to be better off.

One man became very bitter, believing no one else had ever faced such terrible afflictions. In a dream, everyone he knew came and laid down their burdens. The complainer was told he could exchange his burden for any one of the others. But after seeing all the problems of his neighbors, he was glad to pick up his own again.

Until we know about other people's hidden hurts, we may feel cheated, but nobody is exempt from trials and tribulations.

Sometimes we may look ahead in fear and say, "What if?" We manufacture unforeseeable negative situations and worry about things that will never happen.

Once, a young girl was sitting by the road crying. When a helpful friend questioned her, she explained, "Well, I just got to thinking: What if I grow up and get married, and what if I have a baby? And what if it's a boy, and what if our country goes to war, and what if my son has to fight, and what if he is killed?"

That sounds ridiculous since nobody can see the future. Imagining the worst possible scenarios robs us of the joy of the present.

83: Trash, Trinkets, or Treasures?

A sign on a souvenir shop read, "Trash, Trinkets, or Treasures!" That could also serve as a summary of life's choices.

Trash

These life choices are nonproductive and, in fact, destructive. They have an animal-like existence that emphasizes sensual pleasures.

Trash means rubbish, garbage, debris, and worthless clutter. Are you caught up in gossip, criticisms, and negatives? Do you spend time on perversions and violence and evildoing? The writer of Proverbs said, "Lying lips conceal hatred, and whoever utters slander is a fool. When words are many, transgression is not lacking" (Prov 10:18–19).

Paul said, "Have nothing to do with profane and foolish tales" (1 Tim 4:7).

He also said, "Put away from you all bitterness and wrath and anger and wrangling and slander" (Eph 4:31).

Trinkets

These choices aren't evil, but they aren't really good. People who live at this level spend their time and money and energy on trivial pursuits. They are occupied with things that have no real value.

Trinkets mean baubles, trifles, toys, and cheap counterfeits. Are you interested in sensationalism and materialism? Do the rich and famous intrigue you? The writer of Ecclesiastes said, "The lover of money will not be satisfied with money, nor the lover of wealth with gain. This also is vanity" (Eccl 5:10).

Haggai said, "You have sown much and harvested little; you eat, but you never have enough; you drink, but you never have your fill; you clothe yourselves, but no one is warm; and you that earn wages earn wages to put them into a bag with holes" (Hagg 1:6).

Treasures

People who live at this level are concerned with eternal matters. Jesus spoke to this issue when he said, "Do not lay up for yourselves treasures on earth, where moth and rust consume and where thieves break in and steal, but store up for yourselves treasures in heaven, where neither moth nor rust consumes and where thieves do not break in or steal. For where your treasure is, there your heart will be also" (Matt 6:19–21).

Treasure means valuables, essentials, necessities, and things with eternal qualities. Are you committed to truth and permanent achievement? Paul said, "Whatever is true, whatever is honorable, whatever is just, whatever is pure, whatever is pleasing, whatever is commendable, if there is any excellence and if there is anything worthy of praise, think about these things" (Phil 4:8).

"Set your minds on the things that are above, not on the things that are on earth" (Col 3:2).

84: Unanswered Prayers

Why are some of our prayers not answered in the way we expect? There may be good reasons. Suppose a child sees a bike at a yard sale. He begs his dad to buy it. Now, the father loves the child, and he really wants him to have a bike. Even so, there are three very good reasons why he may not grant his son's request.

1. *"Not yet":* This child may be too young to handle a bike. He may need to be a few years older in order to reach the pedals.

2. *"Not here":* The family may live in a dangerous neighborhood where it isn't safe to ride. The child could be hit by a speeding car.

3. *"Not best":* The father may have already bought a new and better bike for the child's birthday next month.

So when prayers are unanswered, God may be saying "not yet!" because we're not mature enough to handle the situation.

Or he may be saying "not here!" because this may not be the right place or the right circumstances.

Or he may be saying "not best!" because there is a better blessing in a different area.

John said, "If we ask anything according to his will, he hears us" (1 John 5:14).

85: The Upside-Down Gospel

Jesus truly turned the world's moral and religious world upside down. We often fail to recognize the shocking view of life that Jesus advocated.

1. *He elevated the poor over the rich.* In that culture people believed wealth indicated God's approval. Yet Jesus said, "It is easier for a camel to go through the eye of a needle than for someone who is rich to enter the kingdom of God" (Matt 19:24). His parable of the rich man and Lazarus was not told to provide a description of hell, but rather to show that riches are futile and poor individuals are loved by God.

2. *He elevated the younger over the older.* The first born was considered as most important and usually received the majority of the inheritance. But in the parable of the prodigal son, Jesus depicted the younger as being cherished by his heavenly Father (see Luke 15).

3. *He elevated a woman over a man.* Women were not respected. They had few rights and were not allowed even to touch a man in public. Yet Jesus defended a sinful woman to Simon, saying, "[This woman] bathed my feet with her tears and dried them with her hair.... Her many sins have been forgiven" (Luke 7:44, 47). Jesus also gave women the honor of being the first witnesses of the resurrection.

4. *He elevated ordinary sinners over religious leaders.* Publicans were hated as greedy traitors, and Pharisees were so pious that they even tithed their seeds and refused to eat eggs laid on the sabbath. But Jesus told a parable that changed this perspective, saying the publican went home justified (see Luke 18:10–14).

5. *He elevated heretical Samaritans over orthodox priests.* Samaritans did not worship according to Mosaic laws and Hebrew teachings. They were shunned and despised while the priests and Levites were highly esteemed religious leaders. Yet in his parable Jesus made the "good Samaritan" the hero (see Luke 10).

6. *He elevated an alien Roman military officer over patriotic Hebrews.* To the Jews, Romans were enemies and infidels. Yet Jesus complimented a Roman centurion's faith as being greater than the Israelites' (see Luke 7:9).

7. *He elevated servants over masters.* In those days the caste system was absolute. Masters could punish and even kill their slaves. Yet Jesus said, "The greatest among you will be your servant" (Matt 23:11).

8. *He elevated children over adults.* Jesus said, "It is to such as these that the kingdom of heaven belongs" (Matt 19:14).

Over and over again, Jesus dealt kindly with the "least and lowest" of the population. Jesus even said, "Truly I tell you, the tax collectors and the prostitutes are going into the kingdom of God ahead of you" (Matt 21:31).

Jesus summarized his mission and message by saying, "Some are last who will be first, and some are first who will be last" (Luke 13:30).

That's an upside-down gospel.

86: Using Our Strengths

We can't drastically change our personality, but we can shape and enhance it by discovering and developing our special abilities. We must not neglect our strengths.

One woman said, "When I was asked to bake a cake for the church bazaar, I agreed, even though I hate baking cakes and am not good at it. Everything went wrong. The first cake scorched. The second one fell. At 2:00 a.m., exhausted and angry, I finally managed to piece together a cake. The next day, mine was the only cake that didn't sell. Resentfully, I surveyed the messy posters above the various tables. As a commercial artist I would have enjoyed doing those. Later, when I apologized to the committee chairman for my cake, she sighed as she replied, 'I love baking cakes, but I had to stay up all night making these dreadful posters.'"

We should use our strengths. We should find our niche. We should take advantage of our natural abilities. Peter said, "Serve one another with whatever gift each of you has received" (1 Pet 4:10).

Every person has potential in some area. For example, entertainers are friendly, cheerful, and popular. They have warmth, charm, and enthusiasm. These strengths can make them excellent in public relations, performing and persuading people.

Executives are confident, logical, and productive. They have energy, organizational abilities, and decisiveness. These strengths can make them successful leaders who get things done.

Philosophers are sensitive, persistent, and deep-minded. They have analytical abilities, imagination, and loyalty. These strengths can make them great scientists, writers, and researchers.

Diplomats are easygoing, tactful, and cooperative. They have patience, listening skills, and mediation abilities. These strengths can make them peacemakers, good friends, and helpful followers.

The best advice to anyone seeking a successful career or developing a satisfying lifestyle is to "go with your strengths." Find your talents, interests, and skills. Then choose jobs, volunteer positions, and recreational opportunities that emphasize these special abilities.

87: Using Plan B!

In life there are ideal goals and perfect solutions, but these are seldom reached. Instead, our progress is often determined by our fallback positions. If we can't do what's best, then what's second best? What are our contingency plans?

Many religions advocate either/or decisions. They insist that every action is either absolutely wrong or absolutely right. But that's not true!

Many scriptures tell us of situations that didn't work out at first. But God is never foiled! Failure is never final!

God allowed Moses to choose second best when he refused to lead and speak for his people. He compromised by sharing the task with his brother Aaron.

God allowed contingency plans in religious rituals. The scriptures say, "You shall bring to the LORD, as your penalty for the sin that you have committed, a female from the flock, a sheep or a goat.... But if you cannot afford a sheep, you shall bring to the LORD, as your penalty for the sin that you have committed, two turtledoves or two pigeons.... But if you cannot afford two turtledoves or two pigeons, you shall bring as your offering for the sin that you have committed one-tenth of an ephah of choice flour" (Lev 5:6, 7, 11).

Of course it would be wonderful to be able to make enormous contributions, but if you can't give thousands, give hundreds. If you can't give hundreds, give what you can!

Preparing for contingencies doesn't show lack of faith. It shows prudence and wisdom. When David confronted Goliath, he prepared for the worst. He chose five stones instead of just one (see 1 Sam 17:39–40, 48–49).

Paul settled for "even so" and learned to live with his thorn in the flesh, saying, "I appealed to the Lord about this, that it would leave me, but he said to me, 'My grace is sufficient for you'" (2 Cor 12:8).

Now, Paul wanted good health. He didn't get it; even so, he served.

Cervantes was in prison; nevertheless, he wrote Don Quixote.

Winston Churchill was called hopeless in school and flunked sixth grade; nevertheless, he became a great statesman.

Franklin D. Roosevelt was struck down with polio; nevertheless, he became the only president to be elected to four terms.

Albert Einstein was labeled a slow learner; nevertheless, he changed physics and science forever.

When success is impossible, a dedicated Christian will say, "I may not be rich; nevertheless, I'll be generous with what I have. Remember the widow's mite?"

A dedicated Christian will say, "I may have made a lot of mistakes; nevertheless, God isn't concerned with my past. He's concerned with my future."

At best, life is hard. Each of us has problems, disabilities, and handicaps. If we succeed in life, we will have to do it in spite of our obstacles. We may have to settle for second best. We may have to struggle on, even so. We may have to achieve our purposes from a "nevertheless" position. But great things have been accomplished by those who use plan B!

Once, an artist saw his friend spill something on her favorite scarf, leaving a permanent stain. Immediately, he said, "Don't throw it away. Let me take it." When he returned it a few days later, the stain had not been removed. That was impossible. Instead, the creative man had integrated the ugly splotch into an overall design with symmetry and beauty. The scarf was stained, but he gave it a second-best option. It was damaged; even so, it was salvaged for use. It wasn't the same; nevertheless, it was a thing of beauty.

88: Wash-Basin Religion

Once, a single mom hired a local fellow to do a small task. He did a good job but then refused payment, saying, "Ma'am, I have a 'wash-basin religion'!"

When she questioned him, he smiled and said, "Our preacher read the scripture about Jesus taking a basin and washing his disciples' feet. I think he meant for us to serve each other. So I always do one repair job free of charge, and when the customer asks me why, I give my Christian witness."

Yes, as Christians, we're saved to serve.

Some people avoid service by saying, "I just don't feel like it. It would be hypocritical to give money or teach those kids or do that good deed if I don't really want to do it. If my heart's not in it, I'd better just forget it."

But that's not true. What if your baby cries for food and you're tired or sick? You don't feel like getting up in the cold to heat a bottle, but you do it because it's the right thing to do. It's your responsibility. It's your duty! We don't have to feel like it to do good deeds.

Other people avoid service by saying, "It's not my problem." Now, each person does have certain gifts and abilities, but if you see a man fall in a ditch, God expects you to help him out instead of saying, "I just don't have the gift of mercy" or "I'm not trained for ditch rescues."

A good motto is this: "If you see a need that you can fill, then that's your calling."

Other people avoid service by saying, "I don't have much to offer." They claim that their little contributions wouldn't be useful. But that's not true either.

A legend tells of a traveler who comes to a town where everyone complains that they are starving and nobody has food. The wanderer insists stone soup could solve their problem. He sets a large pot over a fire in the square and fills it with water. Then he places a stone in the pot and instructs the people to go home and bring back whatever small contribution they have to flavor the stone. One brings a carrot, another a potato, someone else a turnip, and before long there is enough bubbling stew to feed everybody.

Likewise, most of us have more resources than we think we do. If we work together, we can fill needs and solve problems.

Each person's level of responsibility is different. Jesus said, "From everyone to whom much has been given, much will be required, and from the one to whom much has been entrusted, even more will be demanded" (Luke 12:48).

We must use what we have.

If you want to make a difference in the lives of those around you, you don't have to drop gospel tracts from an airplane or display a huge "Jesus Saves" flag in your front yard.

Jesus did a small service by washing dirty feet, and he commanded us to do small services. If you practice a "wash-basin religion," you can serve people and spread the gospel by what you do. James said we must show our faith by our good works (see Jas 2:14–18).

89: We Are Witnesses

The scripture says, "You will be my witnesses…to the ends of the earth" (Acts 1:8). All Christians are witnesses, and the witness of common, ordinary individuals is just as important as the witness of famous evangelists and preachers. Everyone has heard of Peter. But Andrew, his brother, is not as well known. Yet Peter might never have become a disciple without the witness of Andrew. The scripture says the first thing Andrew did was to find his brother, Peter. Then Andrew took Peter to Jesus (John 1:40–42).

Both the Bible and history are full of obscure witnesses who made a difference. Stephen had a great witness. He was one of the first "deacons" of the church and became the first Christian martyr. Like Jesus, he offered forgiveness to his murderers. A man who watched his execution was Saul of Tarsus. The death disturbed him and no doubt led to his conversion on the road to Damascus (see Acts 6 and 7).

When Paul preached in Athens, he was ridiculed. He thought he had utterly failed in Athens, but he hadn't. A member of the council named Dionysius had heard him and became a believer (see Acts 17:34). According to legend, Dionysius later became pastor of the church at Athens.

A joy of Christian witnessing is that you can never know the full influence of your witness. In your home, church, community, and nation you are often asked to complete tasks or contribute resources. Before you refuse or accept half-heartedly, remember this is the Lord's work.

God uses human hands to achieve divine purposes. Instead of sending angels to Nineveh, he sent Jonah. Instead of striking Goliath with lightning, he let David use a sling. Instead of turning stones into bread, he allowed a little boy to share his lunch. God always uses people! The most thrilling thought in the world is that God actually lets you and me carry out plans that affect eternity. There's a legend that when Jesus ascended to heaven, the angel Gabriel met him and said, "I hear that you died for mankind. That's great news! Does everyone know about it?"

Jesus replied, "Oh, no! Just a few. But I told them to tell others."

Gabriel was astonished. "But, Master, what if they don't? What if they get busy and forget?"

The Lord answered, "Then I died in vain. I have no other plan!"

90: What Do We Really Want?

Everyone has unmet needs, frustrated desires, and unexpressed longings. But most of us are unaware of these emotions. Instead, we wait in silent desperation for someone to come along and make things right. Parents fail us. Spouses fail us. Friends fail us. They fail us because they are also needy and unaware. God knows our needs. Jesus said, "Your Father knows what you need before you ask him" (Matt 6:8).

God will also supply our needs. Paul said, "My God will fully supply every need of yours according to his riches in glory in Christ Jesus" (Phil 4:19).

So what do we really want?

1. *We want to be nurtured.* Living things must be fed. Each of us wants to say, "Give me the necessary resources to survive! Provide for me!"

2. *We want to be protected.* Security is essential from birth. Each of us wants to say, "Be concerned about my welfare! Take care of me!"

3. *We want to be accepted.* Rejection is devastating. Each of us wants to say, "Like me just as I am. Don't abandon me!"

4. *We want to be healed.* Wounds and diseases make us vulnerable. Each of us wants to say, "Keep me from hurting! Help me to be strong again."

5. *We want to be understood.* False assumptions cause problems. Each of us wants to say, "See things from my viewpoint! Please know me."

6. *We want to be fulfilled.* Emptiness is miserable. Each of us wants to say, "Make my life complete. Give me meaning and purpose."

7. *We want to be supported.* Standing alone is scary. Each of us wants to say, "Take my side on crucial issues. Be with me against my adversaries."

8. *We want to be approved.* Feeling inadequate demoralizes us. Each of us wants to say, "Tell me I'm okay. Validate my beliefs."

9. *We want to be admired.* No one has enough self-esteem. Each of us wants to say, "Notice me. Compliment me."

10. *We want to be appreciated.* Being taken for granted leaves us resentful. Each of us wants to say, "Be grateful for my presence. Thank me for my assistance."

11. *We want to be needed.* Being idle makes us feel worthless. Each of us wants to say, "Ask me for favors. Lean on me when things get tough."

12. *We want to be loved.* This is a combination of all the others. Each of us wants to say, "Show me that I matter. Cherish my specialness." Only God can provide such unconditional love. John said, "We have known and believe the love that God has for us" (1 John 4:16). If we feel loved, our needs will be met. Our desires will be gratified, and our longings will be satisfied.

91: What Is Love?

As We Have Been

Paul said, "God proves his love for us in that while we still were sinners Christ died for us" (Rom 5:8).

It's encouraging that God can love us at our worst. The prodigal son was not told he had to clean up before he would be accepted. He was not forced to apologize. He was not punished for his sin.

Jacob was a liar, but he wasn't held to his past. Zacchaeus was a thief, but he wasn't held to his past. Paul was a murderer, but he wasn't held to his past. Neither are we!

Conditional love is love with strings attached.

Love *if* is a bribe. It says, "*If* you are good, I will love you." This kind of love ceases if things change.

Love *because* is a payment. It says, "I love you *because* you did me a favor."

Love *for* is a trade. It says, "I love you *for* taking care of me."

God's grace is different!

As We Are

John said, "If we love one another, God abides in us, and his love is perfected in us.... We have known and believe the love that God has for us. God is love, and those who abide in love abide in God, and God abides in them" (1 John 4:12, 16).

This love and acceptance is complete and permanent. It's not contingent on anything we think, say, or do. Since we have this assurance, we can acknowledge our negative attitudes, our selfish ambitions, and our immature reactions. We can admit our sins. We can be honest. We can grow.

As We Will Be

Paul said, "The one who began a good work among you will continue to complete it" (Phil 1:6).

Once, a young girl argued violently with her father and left home. For weeks her devoted parents spent thousands of dollars trying to locate her. They offered rewards and hired detectives. All to no avail.

Then, one afternoon, when their money and hope were almost gone, the father answered the doorbell to find a dirty, sick, weeping daughter on the front steps.

Now, he might have said, "Oh, it's you at last. Well, it's too late. Our love played out last month. So go back where you came from."

Or he might have said, "Oh, what a mess you are. Go somewhere and get a bath, find some clean clothes, and take some medicine for that cough. After that, we may be willing to discuss things."

Or he might have said, "You certainly look awful, but I guess you can come in. If you'll behave, we'll let you stay and keep house for us."

Now, you know he didn't say anything like that. Instead, you know what that father did. He accepted that dirty, sick, weeping daughter instantly, completely, and joyfully, just as she was!

That's grace! God loves us as we have been! He loves us as we are! And he loves us as we will become!

92: What Is the Gospel?

The scripture says, "They…went through villages, bringing the good news" (Luke 9:6). Now, Jesus had not been crucified or resurrected, so what did they preach about? Furthermore, the good news means "gospel." What gospel message could they give during this mission outreach?

Liberation

Jesus said, "You will know the truth, and the truth will make you free" (John 8:32).

A belief that Jesus paid for our sins once and for all became Paul's gospel. It liberated him from the terrible burden of temple sacrifices. It liberated him from the awful guilt of breaking a thousand and one pedantic pharisaical laws. It liberated him from the paralyzing fear of a wrathful God. He expressed this when he said, "For the law of the Spirit of life in Christ Jesus has set you free from the law of sin and of death" (Rom 8:2).

Validation

Jesus said, "You are of more value than many sparrows" (Matt 10:31).

A belief that God accepts us as we are was Zacchaeus's gospel. It validated his worth as a person. It validated his importance as a professional. It validated his efforts to change his behavior. The scriptures say, "[Jesus]…looked up and said to him, 'Zacchaeus, hurry and come down, for I must stay at your house today. So he hurried down and was happy to welcome him" (Luke 19:5–6).

Motivation

Jesus said, "If you love me, you will keep my commandments" (John 14:15).

A belief that we are to act on our faith was James's gospel. It motivated him to morality. It motivated him to witness. It motivated him to service. He said, "Show me your faith apart from your works, and I by my works will show you faith" (Jas 2:18).

Now, each of these individuals emphasized the specific aspect of spirituality that was important to them. So maybe whatever you need to understand in order to change and grow and reach your potential is your good news and your gospel.

93: What Moves Us?

All of us are pushed and pulled by subconscious urges that determine everything we do.

Shame for Who We Are

Feelings of inadequacy, needs for significance, and desires that are selfish cause shame, which leads to coverups and denials. What can we do about shame?

God has the answer: "No one who believes in him will be put to shame" (Rom 10:11).

Guilt for What We Do

Forbidden thoughts, careless words, and hurtful deeds cause guilt, which leads to low self-esteem and expectations of punishment. What can we do about guilt?

God has the answer: "Let us approach with a true heart in full assurance of faith, with our hearts sprinkled clean from an evil conscience" (Heb 10:22).

Fear of What Might Happen

The possibility of losing status, possessions, or life itself causes fear, which leads to anxiety or paralysis. What can we do about fear?

God has the answer: "Perfect love casts out fear" (1 John 4:18).

Anger for What Has Happened

Experiencing deprivation, manipulation, and frustration causes anger, which leads to hostility and rage. What can we do about anger?

God has the answer: "Be angry but do not sin" (Eph 4:26).

Habits of Which We Are Not Aware

Personal conditioning, social influences, and cultural customs cause us to engage in automatic reactions, which lead to irrational and unproductive consequences. What can we do about bad habits?

God has the answer: "You shall not follow a majority in wrongdoing" (Exod 23:2). "If sinners entice you, do not consent" (Prov 1:10). We must become aware of subconscious urges and allow God's spirit to move us!

94: What Should I Feel?

Many evangelicals teach that when individuals are "born again," they experience ecstatic feelings. This expectation can disillusion some people who make sincere commitments and yet have no such feelings. After all, a baby doesn't feel great joy when it's born. Instead, it's the parents and family who rejoice, and that's exactly what the scriptures say happens: "There will be…joy in heaven over one sinner who repents" (Luke 15:7).

The feelings people have when they accept Christ depend partly on their personal temperament. Some individuals are more emotional, and others are more logical. In fact, Jesus says we can come to faith in different ways: "Believe me that I am in the Father and the Father is in me, but if you do not, then believe because of the works themselves" (John 14:11)

Here he says we can simply hear about him and trust in his word, or we can observe and analyze the evidence and draw a conclusion.

The feelings people have also depend on their backgrounds and past teachings. Not all conversions are instantaneous, like flipping a switch to fill a dark room with light. Some conversions are gradual, like observing the dawn. You can't be certain of the exact moment when night becomes day. Fortunately, the method of enlightenment doesn't matter. What matters is the realization that you can now walk in the light.

The feelings people have also depend on how their needs are filled and how their problems are solved. There is a story of four blind men, cured by the Lord, discussing how Jesus heals. One says, "I can tell you from my experience. He simply says, 'Your faith has healed you.'"

Another objects, saying, "No! Faith alone does not suffice. Jesus touches your eyes."

A third adds, "But it must be done twice. If he touches you only once, you see men walking like trees."

A fourth one says, "Nonsense. You're all wrong. Jesus makes mud by spitting on the ground. He puts the mud on your eyes. Then you have to go wash yourself in a certain pool in Jerusalem."

The four former blind men disagreed and formed four different denominations. But Jesus gathered them together and said, "I have healed you all, each one in a different way. Instead of arguing, wouldn't it be better for you to unite in a spirit of gratitude? Am I not free to heal each person as I see fit?"

Since all conversions are different, there is no one particular feeling that follows it. However, several changes do occur in a new Christian's life.

1. *There is usually a quiet sense of relief and peace.* Jesus said, "Come to me, all you who are weary and are carrying heavy burdens, and I will give you rest" (Matt 11:28).

2. *A converted person has a desire to please God and be productive.* Christians get joy from sharing their faith and doing God's work. Paul said, "We speak, not to please mortals but to please God" (1 Thess 2:4).

3. *Our attitude toward others is different.* John said, "We know that we have passed from death to life because we love the brothers and sisters" (1 John 3:14a).

No matter how right a person's belief system is or how moral a person's behavior is, if he doesn't have a genuine love and concern for people, he's not a Christian. John said, "Whoever does not love abides in death" (1 John 3:14b).

So it's not certain ecstatic feelings that are important. We can't depend on feelings to prove our salvation. It's the inner peace, the desire to please God, and our love for others that give us the assurance of our salvation.

95: What the World Needs Now!

Our world today is a dangerous place. It's full of hatred and violence. It's polarized and angry. We desperately need leaders who have depth of integrity and wisdom.

Fortunately, Jesus gave us guidelines for developing such character and behavior. He also lived a life that exemplified such character and behavior.

1. *Jesus never retaliated against personal attacks.* He said, "Do not resist an evildoer.... Love your enemies" (Matt 5:39, 44)

2. *Jesus never tried to stir up animosity by pitting different groups against each other.* He said, "Blessed are the peacemakers, for they will be called children of God" (Matt 5:9).

3. *Jesus never used language that hurt or ridiculed others.* He said, "On the day of judgment you will have to give an account for every careless word you utter" (Matt 12:36)

4. *Jesus never rejected any individual or group of people.* He said, "Anyone who comes to me I will never drive away" (John 6:37). "People will come from east and west, from north and south, and take their places at the banquet in the Kingdom of God" (Luke 13:29).

5. *Jesus never bragged or put others down.* He said, "Whoever wants to be first must be last of all and servant of all" (Mark 9:35). "All who exalt themselves will be humbled" (Matt 23:12).

6. *Jesus never promoted or extolled wealth or power.* He said, "Do not store up for yourselves treasures on earth" (Matt 6:19). "It will be hard for a rich person to enter the kingdom of heaven" (Matt 19:23).

7. *Jesus never used exaggerated language or stretched the truth.* He said, "Let your word be 'Yes, yes' or 'No, no'; anything more than this comes from the evil one" (Matt 5:37).

8. *Jesus never condemned or punished other people.* He said, "Do not judge, so that you may not be judged. For the judgment you give will be the

judgment you get" (Matt 7:1–2). "Do to others as you would have them do to you" (Luke 6:31).

9. *Jesus never approved of self-righteousness.* He said the only man who went home justified was the one who admitted his mistakes and apologized, saying, "God, be merciful to me, a sinner" (Luke 18:13).

These are the standards we're to use in evaluating ourselves and others. Do we measure up? Do our leaders measure up? We must strive to live by Christian principles if we expect our nation to be blessed!

96: What to Do with Hostility

Everyone is hostile at times, but how we handle it is what's important.

1. *We can repress it!* People who repress their hostility paste on a happy face while they seethe inside. They swallow resentments until they turn into bitterness. Unfortunately, buried hostilities multiply! They also come up later as explosive bombs at inappropriate times. The scripture says, "Lying lips conceal hatred, and whoever utters slander is a fool" (Prov 10:18).

2. *We can obsess about it!* People who obsess about their hostilities constantly think about real or imagined slights and criticisms. They talk about them to friends and strangers. They magnify them. They twist every social reaction into a personal slur. Unfortunately, dwelling on a problem exacerbates it and prolongs its effects. The scripture says, "A perverse person spreads strife, and a whisperer separates close friends" (Prov 16:28).

3. *We can assess it!* We can't control other people's actions, but we can control our reactions. Nobody can put us down without our permission. Separating real from imagined attacks is productive. Paul says, "Put away from you all bitterness and wrath and anger and wrangling and slander, together with all malice" (Eph 4:31).

4. *We can express it!* People who express their hostilities usually defuse them. Verbalizing a situation gives us new perspectives. If we can talk about something, we are able to work through it. "Saying it" can help us avoid "fighting it." Solomon says, "Whoever speaks the truth gives honest evidence, but a false witness speaks deceitfully" (Prov 12:17).

5. *We can confess it!* People who confess their hostilities and accept responsibility for them are able to change their reactions and behaviors accordingly. The psalmist said, "I confess my iniquity; I am sorry for my sin" (Ps 38:18).

If you have hostility—and if you're a human being on this planet, you do!—don't repress it or obsess about it. Instead, assess it, express it, and confess it. If you do that, the hostility will become manageable.

97: Whited Sepulchers

Solomon advocates moderation, saying, "Give me neither poverty nor riches" (Prov 30:8).

"Do not be too righteous, and do not act too wise.... Do not be too wicked, and do not be a fool" (Eccl 7:16).

He knows that almost anything pushed too far becomes destructive. You can identify "overzealous" people because they develop these traits:

1. *Intolerance:* There is one way to do everything! My way! Good people agree with me; bad people disagree with me!

2. *Absolutism:* Everything is good or evil. There are no mixtures or neutrals. Every question has one clear, precise, final answer! Every word has one specific, definite meaning!

3. *Rigidity:* Change is bad! Flexibility is weakness! Compromise is sinful! New thoughts are threatening! My mind's made up, so don't confuse me with facts!

4. *Anti-reason:* Thinkers are suspect. Education should be indoctrination. Truth is already known, so exploration and discovery lead to heresy!

5. *Externalization:* Other people or outside forces cause things. The enemy, Satan, or ideological conspirators are lurking everywhere, so I'm not responsible!

6. *Blind obedience:* My supreme allegiance is to a great, unquestioned authority. Submissiveness is a virtue. I've sold out to a dictator, and everyone else must sell out too in order to validate my stance.

7. *Repressiveness:* Since any deviation in lifestyle threatens me, exact, traditional, stereotyped roles must be maintained.

8. *Ethnocentricity:* My race, my denomination, and my country are right! Others are wrong! People who aren't like me aren't to be trusted!

9. *Paranoia:* Since I judge others, I assume others judge me; therefore, I'm suspicious and defensive. I think they are out to get me! I feel persecuted and take pride in my martyrdom!

10. *Infallibility:* I must be invincible; therefore, I blame my own slipups on the opposition group, an evil spirit, or a sinful world!

11. *Power worship:* Inner worth and self-confidence are not valid, so I must seek outside approval. I need titles, plaques, offices, and the overt symbols of success.

These attitudes assure conflicts and destructive consequences.

98: Why Am I Mad?

"I'm just so mad, and I don't know why!"

"I overreacted to that statement, and I don't know why!"

"I got furious when he did that, and I don't know why!"

Have you ever felt that way? Well, there's always a reason, but the real reason may be hidden far back in your past. It may be something that happened when you were a child. In that case, you had no words to explain the incident, so you have no conscious memory of it. Nevertheless, you have a deep and powerful emotional memory, and when something happens now to trigger that emotional memory, you feel again all the suppressed pain and rage that you felt when you experienced the original event.

The trigger may be a word, a facial expression, a tone of voice, a gesture, a scent, an object, or almost anything. Unfortunately, the trigger that awakens the dormant emotion doesn't give you a rational explanation, and that creates mental chaos. Your mind can't tolerate the uncertainty. It must have rational explanations for all emotional reactions. Therefore, when we feel angry for no known reason, we usually "find a reason" in the form of some nearby person or current event. Then we proceed to project our unexplained anger onto these innocent scapegoats.

Blaming others for our misery, however, is totally unproductive and destructive. We hurt them needlessly and then feel guilty because, subconsciously, we know we're projecting. Furthermore, we never get to the root of the problem because we've "copped out" at a superficial level.

This can be a serious mistake because anger causes many personal and relationship conflicts. The scripture gives grave warnings about this: "One who is quick-tempered acts foolishly" (Prov 14:17).

"Make no friends with those given to anger, and do not associate with hotheads, lest you learn their ways and entangle yourself in a snare" (Prov 22:24–25).

"Put away from you all bitterness and wrath and anger and wrangling and slander, together with all malice" (Eph 4:31).

When you feel angry without justification, when you overreact and make mountains out of molehills, or when you let someone rub you the wrong way for no reason, you're probably being triggered by past hurts. To solve that problem, you must not deny the feeling. You must not explode and project your anger onto others. Instead, follow these steps:

1. Become aware of your emotions.
2. Analyze them as to rationality.
3. Trace them back to your childhood situation.
4. Try to "feel them" as a child would feel them.
5. Discuss them with someone.

These suggestions can help you discover why you are mad. More importantly, they can help you defuse your anger by recognizing the triggers!

99. Why Do Adults Say *No*?

A toddler said, "Cows say, 'moo, moo'; ducks say, 'quack, quack'; mommies say, 'no, no.'"

He's right. The average child hears the word *no* about forty thousand times before he's ten years old. Why do parents and teachers say no so often? Are they dictators trying to keep young people from having fun? Are they bullies who enjoy throwing their weight around? Are they old-fashioned nerds, totally out of touch with the real world?

Most adults are none of these things. Instead, most of them are caring people with a lot of wisdom. Remember, these aggravating authority figures have already been kids and teenagers. They've walked that path. They know every crook in the road. They've fallen into the potholes and found the dead-end streets. They know about the rough spots. They've seen the dangerous areas.

Of course, modern life is different, but the basic human needs, desires, and temptations do not change. The pace may quicken, and the vocabulary may expand, but love, hate, fear, and guilt feel the same in every generation. Deep universal emotions affect everyone. Moses was once a frightened five-year-old. Caesar was once a rebellious thirteen-year-old. Shakespeare was once an insecure teenager.

If adults really do understand these feelings, then why do they try to limit kids' freedom? They do it because they've felt pains kids haven't felt. They've seen harmful effects kids haven't seen. They've endured the terrible consequences kids haven't experienced. As adults we can look back and realize things kids can't possibly know.

We say, "Don't smoke," not because we want to deny you a pleasant experience, but because we've watched lung cancer patients die.

We say, "Don't drink," not because we're fanatical prohibitionists, but because we've seen wrecks and divorces and abused children.

We say, "Don't do drugs," not because we're against the "rockstar lifestyle," but because we've seen meth addicts and suicides.

We say, "Don't run with the wrong crowd," not because we want to criticize your choice of friends, but because we've seen gangs and mob violence.

We say, "Don't drive fast," not because we're "killjoys," but because we've visited morgues and read obituaries.

We say, "Don't drop out of school," not because we're intellectual snobs, but because we've seen unemployment lines and welfare checks.

Now, it's true that we may overreact. Not everyone who smokes a cigarette dies of lung cancer. Not everyone who drinks a beer becomes an alcoholic. Not everyone who uses marijuana becomes an addict. Not everyone who has an undesirable friend becomes a criminal. Not everyone who drives eighty miles per hour becomes a paraplegic. No, not everyone, but the possibilities—and in many cases the probabilities—are there!

As adults we have seen the tragic results of a little irresponsible "fun." We are able to weigh a momentary whim against a lifetime of regret and realize the risk is just not worth it! You only have one life and no second chances when it's gone. We love you so much.

Yes, we may go to extremes. We may paint things worse than they are. We may say *no* too often. But if we do, it's because we care so very much!

An observer watching a gardener attacking insects said, "Man, you must really hate those creatures!"

"No," the gardener replied. "It's not that I hate bugs so much. It's just that I love roses so much more!"

Likewise, it's not that we hate fun so much. It's just that we love kids so much more.

100: You Are Valuable!

You are valuable because God made you! As a little child once said, "God don't make no junk!" When Moses had his moment of truth, God said, "The place on which you are standing is holy ground" (Exod 3:5).

Now, that dirt and that bush were not endowed with special divine attributes. The place was holy ground because that's where Moses met God. God is still saying that to us. The place where you stand is holy ground. It's holy ground because that's where God is! The scripture says, "Do you not know that you are God's temple and that God's Spirit dwells in you?" (1 Cor 3:16).

The next verse is even more awesome: "If anyone destroys God's temple, God will destroy that person. For God's temple is holy, and you are that temple" (1 Cor 3:17).

Now, most of us would never think of destroying or desecrating or vandalizing a church building, yet we think nothing of desecrating our bodies and our minds and our spirits. And these make up the temple of God.

1. *We can desecrate our bodies.* We do this through poor eating habits, lack of exercise, promiscuous behavior, alcohol and drug use. There are many ways to destroy our health and dissipate our energy. Paul said, "The body is not meant for sexual immorality but for the Lord.... Do you not know that your bodies are members of Christ?... Do you not know that your body is a temple of the Holy Spirit within you, which you have from God?... Therefore glorify God in your body" (see 1 Cor 6:13–20).

2. *We can desecrate our minds.* We do this through negative thoughts, lack of knowledge, false information, pornography, and superstition. There are many ways to ruin our intellect and abuse our mental abilities.

Once, a teenager was begging to go to an X-rated movie. That evening, when her mother was preparing supper, she dumped the potato peelings and other garbage into the bowl of salad. Her daughter was horrified. "Mom! Why on earth did you do that?"

"Well," her mother replied, "I thought since you were willing to put garbage in your mind, it wouldn't bother you to put garbage in your stomach!"

Paul understood this. He advised, "Whatever is true, whatever is honorable, whatever is just, whatever is pure, whatever is pleasing, whatever is commendable, if there is any excellence and if there is anything worthy of praise, think about these things" (Phil 4:8).

3. *We can desecrate our spirit.* We do this through neglecting worship and prayer, living stressful lifestyles, and having hostile attitudes. There are many ways to defile our character and waste our talents. The contamination of our spirit develops so gradually that we may not realize what's happening until it's too late.

Some people say, "Oh, let the boys and girls sow their wild oats." But the scripture doesn't agree with that. It says, "Remember your creator in the days of your youth, before the days of trouble come and the years draw near when you will say, 'I have no pleasure in them'" (Eccl 12:1–2).

God expects our best at every stage of life.

A pastor once baptized an old man and a young boy. To the elderly convert he said, "I solemnly baptize you in the name of the Father, the Son, and the Holy Spirit."

To the youth he said, "I joyfully baptize you in the name of the Father, the Son, and the Holy Spirit."

When someone asked about the difference, he said, "The old gentleman gave God his heart minus a life. The young boy gave God his heart plus a life."

You are the temple of God. His spirit dwells in you. Don't put anything into your body, mind, or spirit that God wouldn't want to live with. Remember this: "The place where you stand is holy ground."

101: Z Is for Zeal

According to an old English folktale, Little Red Hen lived in a barnyard with her chicks, a duck, a goose, and a pig. One day, Little Red Hen found some grains of wheat. "Look! Look!" she clucked. "Who will help me plant this wheat?"

"Not I," quacked the duck, and he waddled away.

"Not I," honked the goose, and he hurried away.

"Not I," oinked the pig, and he trotted away.

"Then I will plant it myself," said Little Red Hen, and she did!

Later, at harvest time, Little Red Hen cut the wheat. Then she had it milled into flour. She used the flour to make dough for her bread. She baked her bread in an old wood stove.

With each task Little Red Hen asked the duck, the goose, and the pig if they would help. The reply was always, "Not I."

But when the bread came out of the oven, Little Red Hen asked, "Who will help me eat this warm, fresh bread?"

"I will," said the duck.

"I will," said the goose.

"I will," said the pig.

"No you won't," said Little Red Hen. "You wouldn't help me plant the seeds, cut the wheat, grind the wheat, make the dough, or bake the bread. Now my chicks and I will eat this bread ourselves!" And they did!

Paul would have agreed with Little Red Hen. He said, "We gave you this command: Anyone unwilling to work should not eat" (2 Thess 3:10).

This story is an illustration of Jesus's promise: "Well done, good and trustworthy slave; you have been trustworthy in a few things; I will put you in charge of many things" (Matt 25:21).

An anonymous poem reads:

> The church is made up of just two kinds of folks,
> No matter how closely you view it.
> The ones who will talk about what should be done,
> And those who get busy and do it.

1. *We must be concerned.* Jesus emphasized concern over and over again. He criticized the rich man who did not have concern for the beggar,

Lazarus, who lay at his gate. He commended the Samaritan who did have concern for the man who had been robbed. Concern moves us to action.

2. *We must be productive.* A businessman said, "Every time I hear the word lucky applied to a successful person, I think of all the things he did that others in his position wouldn't do, and all the years he had been doing them. When a truck needed to be driven, he drove it. When a package needed to be delivered, he delivered it. He came early and stayed late. He always managed to be in the right place at the right time. People who achieve greatness all seem to have that kind of 'luck.'" They are productive.

3. *We must be committed.* This requires total dedication. Jesus didn't say, "If you act religious, you will have a reward from your Father in heaven" (see Matt 6:1).

We may know all the rules of "religiosity"; we may look the way we think a Christian should look; but if we disregard the hard, daily struggle of being a Christian, God isn't fooled!

We must be willing to say, "I by my works will show you faith" (Jas 2:18).

We are called to be concerned, productive, and committed.

Z is for zeal!

www.ingramcontent.com/pod-product-compliance
Lightning Source LLC
Chambersburg PA
CBHW070937180426
43192CB00039B/2315